zuckerbook

Jerry Zucker Middle School of Science

The Zuckerbook Project

2015/16
volume 3

faculty advisor, CEO
Mr. Erik J. Hilden

internal production
Alex Pretto editor
Kenya Williams copywriter

art department
Jalen Corbin team Leader
David Cattles team member
Jan Patterson team member
Cordell Johnson team member

public relations
Samiyah Frasier public relations lead
Jasmain Jenkins instagram, snapchat
Syncere Washington webmaster, pinterest
Angela Scott twitter, swing position

accounting, management
Alyssa Kapinos chief financial officer

cover art **Joel Orellana**

Published by **The Zuckerbook Project**, 2015/2016 Volume 3,
North Charleston, SC.

The Students of Jerry Zucker Middle School of Science
6401 Dorchester Road, North Charleston, South Carolina 29418
Principal: Jacob Perlmutter

ISBN #: 978-0-692-59235-9

Printed in the United States of America.

Dedication

This work is dedicated to the students
who created each piece that is
contained within these pages.
Their words, their artwork, their spirits
and their energies bring this work to life.
May their voices always be heard.

Community Involvement

Endeavors such as these are evidence of the great things that can
happen when a community pulls together in the face of adversity and
produces a testament to the voices of their children. Without the
support of our community, this would not have been possible, and
without further support, future endeavors may not come to pass.
We have had a lot of support this year, but we can always use more,
as is true of any non-profit activity. If you are interested in donating
to The Zuckerbook Project or are interested in volunteering to help
in any way, please feel free to get in touch. I can be reached at:
erik_hilden@charleston.k12.sc.us or at the following address:

The Zuckerbook Project c/o
Jerry Zucker Middle School of Science
6401 Dorchester Rd. Room 159
North Charleston, SC 29418
843-767-8383 ext. 25614

Acknowledgements

Acknowledging the support of your people can be a complicated task. This is a dicey proposition, for an assortment of reasons that sound paranoid or ridiculous. What if I forget someone? What if I mess up and thank someone for something they didn't do? What if I get a name stuck in my head and cannot remember what they did but know that they need to be included somehow? The mind boggles.

But, knowing that it is a necessary thing, and being all to happy to comply with this tradition, here goes. In advance, I apologize to any-one who did not receive the thanks they are due. These things happen, and I assure you that there was no malice whatsoever in any of those potential omissions. I, being human, simply forgot. Or made a mistake. I am now admitting it, in advance, and hope that this apology will suffice.

They used to give awards for that.

That said, the good people who made this edition of Zuckerbook possible are nothing short of miraculous, and I and the entire staff are excited to include them here.

Mr. Jacob Perlmutter, our esteemed principal, has given us unwaivering support in the midst of his busy schedule, and his allowing us to slim down the class that produces this work has made all of the difference. We will always be grateful for his support, and appreciate his allowing us the autonomy necessary to make this work. Without him, we would not be here, and you would not be reading these words. There is no measure to how appreciative we are, and shall remain.

Mr. Kendall White and **Mr. Alex Maybank** continue to visit frequently, jump in to talk to the students, and give me a much needed mid-morning break. Thank you, gentlemen, as always.

Ms. Bridget Means of **StudioHawk** has contributed countless hours of work designing our identity, choosing artwork, and developing our book from the beginning. There is no measure to our gratitude.

Ms. Nikki Mustipher, Ms. Kelly Macomber, Ms. Angela Taylor, Ms. Elizabeth Gleim, and **Ms. Shorace Guider** continue to provide connections to students that I could never acquire on my own, funnel writing to us that we are all to happy to publish, and support us in other wings of the school. **Ms. Erika Gilly** recommended most of our staff, provided us with outstanding writing, and a great deal of support over the last year, and it is difficult to imagine that we would be where we are today without her. **Ms. Zan Gregory** continues to give us access to student artwork, which is the perfect compliment to student writing and a much appreciated contribution. The entire **faculty and staff of Zucker Middle School** has tolerated our pleas for donations, financial support, and our fundraising activities, and the janitorial staff continues to clean up after us without complaint.

Dr. Clark G. Hilden, who has continued to donate to our cause, deserves special mention for donating large amounts of money and inspiration, support for our students, and mentoring as we go forward in the unchartered waters of small batch publishing. Take a look at his textbook, Uniquely Oregon, if you want an interesting read about a fascinating state created by a dedicated teacher of geography. It is fun to read regardless of your interests. Buy it at **Amazon.com.**

Cynthia A. Hilden also deserves special mention for her large cash donations and ongoing moral support, as well as her mentoring and dedication to teaching writing and reading. She remains an inspiration and a much appreciated supporter of The Zuckerbook Project, and for this we are grateful.

Ms. Sarah Douglas remains a spirit guide on our journey. Her enthusiasm for our students and their work has always been remarkable, and the students that she now teaches are among the most fortunate on the planet. It is my sincere hope that they know what a treasure they have on their hands, and I am proud to call myself her friend and colleague.

Mr. James Brooks helped me whittle down the class size for this school year, has been gracious in his support of what we are doing, and continues to bring us new and talented people, all of whom have contributed, in their own way, to The Zuckerbook Project and the products that we create. We thank him for being here with us, and for having our backs as we go forward with expanding the reach of The Zuckerbook Project.

Mr. Mike Grant and his wife **Brenda** brought us to their church to offer our work to an interested public, and we had the most success-ful day of sales in our history. We were given an opportunity to support a local scholarsship fund with a portion of our sales, my Public Relations Staff was given a chance to try their chops at direct sales, and we moved twenty-seven copies of Zuckerbook in under three hours. We are grateful for that opportunity, and are looking forward to the next fundraiser.

The good people at **Barnes and Noble**, and **Kristin Poplin**, the Community Business Development Manager at their North Charleston store, have afforded us an amazing opportunity. **Ms. Poplin** gave us the information needed to get our work into their stores, and **Barnes and Noble** is the first brick-and-mortar store to carry Zuckerbook. We hope it is the beginning of a long anf fruitful relationship, and are proud to work with them to get our work into the hands of readers in our community and around the United States.

To each of you, thank you. This book is as much for you as the students and communty with which we work.

The Mission of The Zuckerbook Project is, and shall remain, to produce the very highest quality Student Publication of Literary Works intermingled with Visual Art, while Remaining Faithful to the Zucker Middle School Student Experience, and then distribute it to the community, so that our voices may be heard.

Open it and read...

-- Mr. Erik J. Hilden, November 25th, 2015

zuckerbook

Contents

1 Change

Years to Come

Kory Singleton

I stand here
Out on this cluttered road,
Watching cars pass me
As year by year, I grow old.

I used to be ahead of the race,
But then, I stopped and quit.
I settled out of my car,
And let the winds of reality hit.

I use to be so anxious to fill my car up,
Perhaps all my first place ribbons were
Obtained by luck.
Cause now, I've let someone steal my car.
I don't need it anymore, no more hiding scars.

When I came to the dealership
Where every other car would go,
I would feel enlightened
To be at the top, so...

Where has this sudden
Emptiness come from?
A loss of intuition,
Or a winning of my own drum?

Ba dum, ba dum, ba dum,
Up and down this street, I go,
Marching to the beat of my own drum,
Not the driver inspectors own...

I'm done with that.

I'm done with the DMV.
I'm down with trying to get a license.
I lost my will to drive,
So I've stopped fighting.

I stand here,
Out on this cluttered road,
Watching cars pass me
As year by year, I grow old.

Happy?

Samiyah Frasier

Someone said to me
"Be happy."
"Be you."
"Enjoy it."

I would crack a smile.
Does it bring me joy?
I would clap my hands.
Does it give me praise?

I would stomp my foot.
Does it bring music to my ears?
I would close my eyes.
Am I being Baptized?

I would slowly breathe.
Am I being released?
I would wake up all over again.
Am I happy?

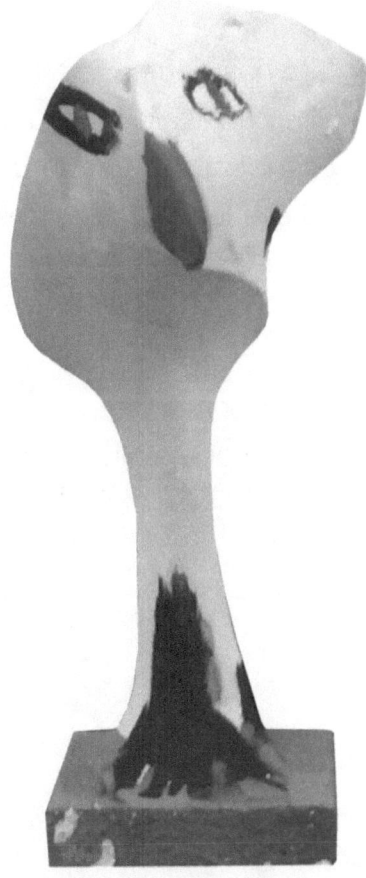

Change Is Oh So Beautiful

Jakayla Gordon

Change is amazing.
It is everywhere,
But no one really cares.

Oh the beauty of change,
The beautiful natural flowers grow.
Tall and pretty on the mountain range,
As we play in the winter snow.

She has gotten so tall,
She can finally reach the stove.
She looks out the window,
As she leans against the wall,
She stares at the summer orange flower grove.

Change is Amazing,
It is everywhere,
But no one really cares.

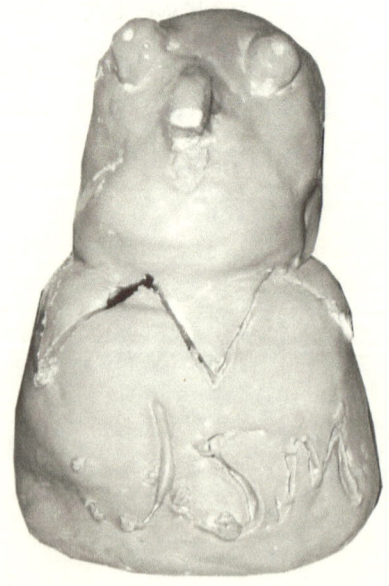

Who I Am

Christina Smith

I sit in the sublime serenity of the quiet.
Every thought there can ever be,
Including the ruthlessly painful memories,
All of them rush to me,
As if I were on an excruciatingly painful diet.

I sit in the quiet, blank white room of my mind.
But yet that room is overflowing.
With velvety memories glowing.
From the little seed in the concrete that kept growing,
To any thought you would ever want to find.

I am so frivolously insouciant,
And yet so anxiously solicitous.
Creating a prodigious amount of thought.
I am susceptible to most every detail and influence,
Which is why I have no idea who I am.

Starbucks

Ca'shun Barr

The leaves fall ever so gently,
The movement as precise as a ballet dancer,
Into a pile as big as Mount Everest.

The mixture of emotions.
The feel of the cold air.

The children's laughter,
The craze of the costumes,
The trick or treat,
The amazing taste of candy,
The warm smell of that
Pumpkin spice latte…

Starbucks.

The scarves, coats and transition period,
As all things are dying around this time,
Lying on the cold solid ground.

And I feel left out and overwhelmed.
Only if that one little leaf would yell.

Growing Up

Daisy Cedillo Perez

Change can be bad or good.
It can make your life a disaster.
But you must move on.
Change can also be fun.

When you take your first steps,
And can freely run,
Then you're having your first dance.
You find the one you marry.

Later little people come into your life.
Their lives are put in your hands.
Your little ones grow up.
It can get kinda scary.

The ones you want to protect,
Grow up and move away.
But you know they can't stay.
Now you're on your hospital bed.

They stand by you,
They hold your hand,
The last words you hear,
"I love you."

Change

A'Lanna Ellison

Change is wonderful.
It makes us who we are.
It gives our lives a purpose .

Change is unique.
It is different.
It makes us think differently.

Change is natural.
It makes us who we are.
It happens, and it can be scary.

Change is change.
It happens, no matter what.
It is what we face everyday.

Change is everything!

The Wind is Crazy

Ca'Shun Barr

The wind crazy
Like she's Sharkeisha, he ain't havin' no mo' babies.
I hear his bloody screams as
The wind cries his name, Joaquin.
Come in for a play date.
Let me come out, endure your rain for fame,
As that crazy guy who sat and watched you cry.
Harder and harder the water droplets fall.

Hoping the pain would be gone,
As I stood up for more, I watched and waited
And then did parkour.
Feeling more free than ever, just like a hurricane.
Like K Camp, I'm talking bout that money baby,
Joaquin said again, but less hazy.

As I seen him flick him his wrist real lazy,
This boy tore down a tree.
Funny, thing is he can't count to three.
Now we're all over and done,
Back to you, Shaun.

A Small Difference

Devonte Alston

What makes one little bug
Feel different from the rest of us?
We learn the same stuff
And we all ride the same bus.

Is there a difference?
We've all wanted to destroy some piece of beautiful art
In front of our peers,
Creators of our tears and broken hearts.

I'm not different,
But that's a splendid adjective.
I prefer to be referred to as unique.
That's a pretty unique adjective to be deemed.

Unfortunately,
My philosophy
Is that we are the same,
But in different ways.

I dislike the phrase
I'm not going to say the word hate
That people say that they're way beyond
Their current generation.

Those words that they utter in your head,
Those words to me have no meaning.
Those words I dread,
I just don't believe that those words were said to me.

So many guys who
Haven't graduated high school,
Yet they were the ones who've made poetry cool
The same blonde dude who flunked out of high school.

A guy who didn't even go to college
But left high school with millions of dollars in his pocket.
Anyone who considers themselves beyond their years
Shouldn't be in a place called "here."

For anyone I've offended,
It's only an opinion.
Unless you're too wise to handle a word with TWO N's.
Only wise people know the world and it's contents.

You're not wise.
You're most definitely aren't ignorant.
You're not different,
You just have different opinions.

Who is this?

Zamani Lyde

Who is this person?
(looks in mirror).
I've been torn between a childish life
And a newly experienced young adult life.

One day it's lipstick and pearls.
The next day it's pigtails and curls.

My mind and body are even confused just like me.
One day I'm stuffing tissue in my TRAINING bra,
The next day I want tissue out of my ACTUAL breast

I head outside to catch this bus
To start the FIRST day of eighth grade.
Although, I am having an internal conflict
With myself.

I must go out and face my fellow peers.
I head on in.
A tight red and black striped tank top
With my favorite boyfriend jeans
And my brown gladiator sandals.

"Girl you boobs are HUGE," my friend Shawna says,
Very loud. Her intentions I don't know.
"Girl, I know I'm a D now," I say excitedly,
Although I'm very SHY about my BIG boobs.

Seeing that now I would be considered "stacked."
"When Evan sees you he won't be able to
Take his eyes off you, your boobs especially,"
Shawna says with a loud cackle for a laugh.

"Girl, ain't no one checking for Evan,"
I say, even though I wanted him badly.
"Yes you are you know you still want him,
Don't trip, please," Shawna says.

Eeekkk, the sound our same old junky,
Broken down bus makes.

We arrive at school 20 minutes later,
While we are only 10 minutes
Away from our school.

I enter into my HR, my teacher Mrs.Ruddy.
The very BORING honors teacher.
I survive all 5 classes, even Mr. Halloway's class.
He's the English honors teacher.

His breath kills a whole population of people
When he says one word.
He also has this very weird bald head,
Weird because it has a shine to it
As if he applies gloss to it every day.

I just want to touch it
and see if it's greasy,
but of course I never will.

Shortly, after Mr. Hallowway's class is over,
It's time to go home.
We all get off the bus
even Evan, my uhhh Ex!!

"Y'all see Eddy Lee?"
Brian a tall, fat, brown-skinned boy says.
Eddy Lee was a mentally challenged boy
who has a heart of gold. Pure gold.

"Yeah what about him?" Shawna asks.
"He's eating ice cream, y'all wanna have some fun?"
"Yeah," they all say in unison. Everyone except me.

We all walk over to Eddy Lee,
Where he is sitting on his porch,
Eating a chocolate fudge ice cream bar
Thats is dripping on his chin and shirt.

"Smelly Eddy, smelly Eddy," Brian says.
Shortly after, everyone joins in.
Eddy looks puzzled at first.
Then he begins to cry.

He cried a cry that hurt my heart horribly.
I finally get sick of the torment.
I push my way to the front and yell
"STOP IT, y'all need to stop bullying him.
Y'all don't want Eddy's brother to come out here, so leave!"

Everyone looks confused at first,
because usually I would stand by
and just watch it.

Not today.

Everyone begins to leave while saying rude remarks.
"Alright Elaine, stay with the retard, we out,"
Brian says as he throws up his ashy fingers
to create a peace sign.
I think to myself, yeah I'll stay with Eddy,
my sweet friend Eddy.

I've now found my place in the world.
I know my conflict isn't over,
but I think I can now understand some of it,
and grasp onto one of the handles of life.

2 Seasons

Falling Leaves

Julia Guo

A spectrum of yellow, orange and red,
Loathing the fantasy of how fall is,
Loving the rain and floods I'm in.

Oh The Rain, Oh The Rain

Jemiell Laguitao

Rain.
Rain rain.
You're falling down
Again and again.

You keep hitting the ground,
Rain rain.
Your drops are icy col
Again and again.

You keep hitting,
its not getting old.
Rain rain.
You make things mucky
Again and again.

Its a disgust,
Rain rain,
You don't do much
Again and again.

Just as if you were dust,
Rain rain,
I know your kind
again and again.

You make our world chime,
Rain rain.
Please dont go away
Again and again.

Please skip school
for just one
more
day.

Water

Karisma Hamilton

When I first saw him, I took my first step in.
The feeling between my toes, was a beautiful thing.

Shallow.

He looked back at me, and I felt the sparks.
I smiled to myself, and walked two more steps.

Deep.

I first saw his eyes. Such a beautiful sight.
Then followed his smile, a couple more steps.

Deeper.

He got closer and laughed, then grabbed my hand.
He guided me in, a few more steps.

Too deep.

Words filled the air, "He likes her..."
And "He doesn't like you..."
But the only thing I could truly hear,
Is my own heart breaking.

Drowned.

Rain

Keyonne' McKnight

The rain is a beautiful thing.
Most people think it's gloomy and dreary,
But I think the contrary.

Most say they bring up bad memories.
It's nothing but a burden and it ruins my plans.
But no, no, no, I definitely don't.

I think it shines brighter than the sun,
More beautiful than the moon.
It's better than all the things combined together.

For me it does bring up bad memories.
Then it washes it all away,
Sweetly and slowly.

I simply adore the rain
And all its beauty that comes with it.
I proudly embrace it with no regrets

I love the rain and...
There are no ifs, ands, or buts about it.
I really do love the rain.

Strange and Damp Over the Rain

Gage Knueve

Strange and damp over the rain,
We envision desirous rabbits over the fog.

Alas! The lust has fled.
I am entranced behind the vapors.
I bend brilliant men within the water.

Be luminous. They will come,
Strangely misty near them.
I transform black death in the fire.

Be wary! The demon must continue
Wavering, intangible,
Walking out of the world,
Empty hands.

With what regrets
The warrior
Chases his dream,
Wondering why?

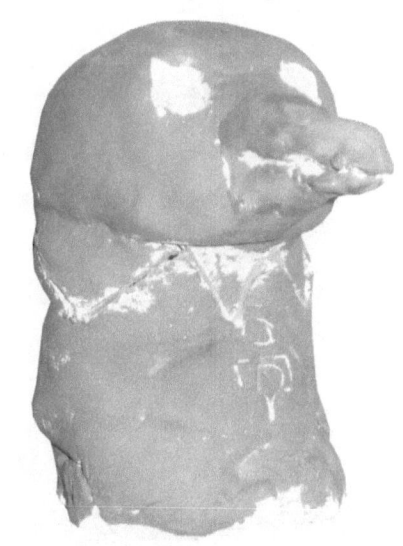

Old Lady

James Aiken

Well, the rain is coming down pretty hard,
But the big news was about an old lady.
Well she thought she could cross
Through a big space of water,
But then went headless.

Through news reports, she told us what happened.
"Well I was going through,then
I dropped my butterscotches.
I bent over to grab them, then my hair fell in the water.
I tried catching it but I fell, good thing this nice
Young man came to help."

That was her response to the incident.
But don't go in those floods,
Or you'll be just like that
Old lady.

It's Almost Over

Godwins Tuyishime

It's almost over.
The cold year of pain,
The hell in the icy room of that man,
Not only that we burn at home like acid rain.

One down, three to go.
May seem like a lot more,
But I ain't done, no,
I got a long way to go, but
I'll breeze my way through,
Though.

I'm tired of the cold winter.
Can't wait for me to be a winner.
To graduate from that stage,
And join my beautiful age

One down, three to go.
I'll keep counting till the end.
Next time, it will be done.
Four down, now it's done.

Why Rain, Why!?

Devonte Alston

Oh my god.
Oh my god.
It's happening again.

Not the blogs,
I'm talking about the rain.
The same weather that happened
In the 6th grade.

They promised us snow.
It was only more rain.
The problem was,
We had to come back on Tuesday.

It's supposed to be a day
Not for relaxation,
But for the same lessons in Springboard
That we learned two springs before.

People were asking me questions.
They were all the same.
Devonte,
It's Friday.
What, are you
Insane?

Insane is this guy's middle name,
Alongside crazy.
That's also what
Everyone is sayin'.

The kind of kid who
Still wants to go to school
Since he has nothing
Else to do.

But instead, all he can do
Is sit around
And watch the rain
Pour all over the ground.
Destroying the green on the leaves.

Like the rain,
This kids' boredom
Has no boundaries.

Wanting to do something,

I'm just a kid
Wanting to make something
Out of nothing.

The Floods

Kenny Coronel

Look there's another drop of rain on the window.
Actually there is a pond of them in my garage.
Nice day to go swimming, right?

Well, school was cancelled yesterday for no reason.
Funny, how we went to school the day it was flooded,
But all I saw yesterday was some nice, fluffy, gray clouds.

Today I see that the ditch in front of my house
Is filled with water.
Usually its filled with leaves.
Honestly what I thought was grass is now water.

I've never seen this happen before here.
Well, I've seen water,
Just not a lot of it in my backyard.

Now my dad doesn't have to worry
About the plants needing water.
I think they have too much right now.

I also saw a dead earthworm today on my front doorsteps.
I thought they loved the rain?
I might be wrong.

Well, at least I wasn't stuck in the house the whole day.
My family and I decided to go to the mall.

Probably not the smartest decision,
Since there were flood warnings scheduled till 8:15 pm.

But we went anyway.
I just stayed in the car
While they went in and got some gifts
For the party which we were going to go to
Later that evening.

While I was in the car,
I was listening to music.
But the thundering, wind, and rain
made the songs sound like a remix.

You could say mother nature was a deejay.

After 20 minutes of listening
To mother nature's deejaying,
My parents came and we left.

On these days,
I rather have my mother driving than my father.
I really never knew that a puddle
Could go up to around seven feet
With my dad driving.

That was nice to know.

Well, we were going to a party.
But are only way of getting there was closed.
There was no road.
Instead, there was a lake.

So we turned back and headed home.
Either way I didn't want to go.
So thank you, Mother Nature!

When we arrived home,
I looked outside to see that the doghouse
Was floating in the middle of the backyard.

That was a nice experience.
My dog was on the porch and
just kept barking at his doghouse.

So thank you Hurricane Joaquin.
Thank you for letting me sit in my house
And watch outside to see what a lake looks like
In my backyard.

Also thank you Mother Nature,
For letting this happen twice in a year.

Also thank you for letting me know
That floods can happen
In North Charleston.

Autumn

Alyssa Kapinos

The third season of the year,
When the green leaves start to fear.
Where we start to embrace,
for the change of weather we have to face.

The flowers start to wilt,
As I start to wrap up in guilt.
The green washes away in a blur,
And the orange comes in to a lure.

The wind comes in to blow away,
The life so that all starts to decay.
The animals start to scurry up food,
Which always come to intrude.

Autumn, the third season of the year,
I am excited and start to cheer.
Kids are running around,
Jumping in leaves which are around.

The third season of the year,
When the green leaves start to fear.
Where we start to face,
For the cold weather we have to face.

Weather or Not

Trey Hensley

It has been a gloomy day all week and it finally started raining Thursday. I got on the bus Thursday afternoon and was told that there wasn't any school tomorrow due to the floods. I had no idea what floods they were talking about until I got home and watched the news. They were talking about catastrophic floods and I was assuming downtown because there was no floods here. There were some puddles but that was it. It continued to rain all day and night as the hours passed on Thursday. I went to sleep thinking about the "floods". Thinking about if it was going to be flooded when I woke up. Thinking about if I was going to be awoken to water in the house. Thinking about the weekend's weather.

I woke up Friday morning to, no rain or floods. I began to think I shouldn't be worried. I woke up are breakfast and just chilled out all day. I honestly didn't do anything Friday. I mean there was nothing I really could do. I was afraid that if I go outside that the rain would just start pouring. At 4-5 o'clock, it started raining. All I could think about was is this what they were talking about because it's not that bad. My grandmother started telling me there was going to be tornadoes and I immediately turned on the news. I automatically assumed when she told me that there isn't going to be tornadoes just thunderstorms and I told her that she needed to calm down and it's not that serious. I had plans to go to a friends house that night so I got packed. My grandmother was just trying to convince me that there's supposed to be tornadoes and stuff and tried her best to keep me here. I didn't care. I kept going on with my weekend. I left at around 5:30. I didn't get soaked but I got drops on my shirt. It's alright though, I had an umbrella. I got to my friends house and it was still raining. I still didn't see any floods. I started on my homework and that was pretty much it for that night.

I woke up the next morning to rain. Rain again. NO TORNADOES. Yup. I got up got a shower and went out to breakfast. The rain kind of messed up our plans because we had to change our routes and everything but it was good. I did see some flooding. Well not really. There were many puddles though. I went home at around 2 o'clock, and layed in my bed to watch the news. I saw all the pictures of the flooding and I assumed it was downtown. I saw some flooding in North Charleston too. I had no idea where some of those places are. I fell asleep to the sounds of the rain. Here I am now doing blogs. I don't see any floods outside but I'm sure there's much more rain to come.

The Waves

Kory Singleton

I like when hair is waved.
I like when people wave.
I like to do the wave.
I like waves.

We took a trip to the pool.
Everything was fine.
The water was cool.
It made me feel alive.

What happened was different
Than what I assumed.
What happened was different
Than what happened at the pool.

My mom said get my cousin.
It was time to go.
Yes, it was time to "go."
Go far, far away.

I jumped in thinking I saw her.
It a beautiful thing.
But I lost my balance in the water.
How is that a thing?

I went under looking for breath.
I started breathing in water.
It filled up my chest.
But why not the rest?

The water was friendly but
For some reason we fought
Like North and South Korea,
Fighting for water during a drought.

If only it were a drought.
Then I would've been fine.
Now I have a memory
I will keep for life.

The waves constantly dragging me
Under the roof of their house.
I was lost and couldn't find the stairs,
Up and out.

I barely made it out.
The doctor said I'd be fine,
But that I'd have a fear of waves,
And feel a chill down my spine.

I know I don't have to rhyme,
It's just my natural instinct.
Like it is for someone to wave
During their first in-synch
Conversation.

Now I hate your hair in a wave.
I hate when people wave.
I hate to do the wave.
I hate waves.

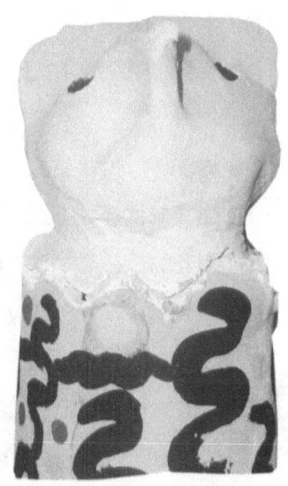

The October Change

Keyonné Mcknight

Look at the leaves
Spiraling around us.
All different colours,
All different personalities.

Leaves are just like people.
We all have different shades of color,
We all have different personalities,
Just like leaves we all start out green.

But as years go by things happen,
People change into something else.
Rather it's good or bad,
Rather it's sad or mad.

Leaves go through the same thing,
Only for them it happens in a matter of months.
They change developing their own colors.
They might be red, brown, orange, or yellow.

The leaf might be a mad red or a passionate red,
It might be a sad brown or an earthly brown,
It might be a bold orange or a warm orange,
It might be a happy yellow or a irritated yellow.

No matter what, leaves are just like us.
Sure, they can't breathe or eat,

Or walk and talk,
We don't even look the same.

But that's not what counts.
Since they can't talk they express what they are
Through color.
They all do it very beautifully too.

We all have one thing in common.
We eventually have to go.
The wind will blow us away,
For the new generation can take over.
Then we'll all become sickly brown.

There's nothing we can do about it.
That's just life and we have to deal with it.
It's depressing and happy at the same time.
You get to see the next generation but you're dying.

Life must go on.
The world must go on,
And time stops for no one.
I'm proud to be just like a leaf.

South Carolina Rain

Quinton Adams

Wow, it's a rainy day. Days like this that are great.
I love the rain, so keep your opinion
Because I don't care what you say.
I don't know why I like the rain so much
Maybe it's pure love, or even fate.
Some say that a dog is a man's best friend,
But not if that dog is slain.

Rain on me, rain, rain, drop.
Man to self or man to nature, oh boy do I love rain.
Rain is a beautiful wonder of the world,
Such an amazing sound out could make a heart stop.

So many things in the world that bring pain.
I just think of the gift from God and hope that it rains.
It is just amazing and something special is sent.
Rain is great, wet, and magnificent.

Rain is like a big wet kiss from a dog.
It's the best feeling ever.
Never did like smoke nor did I like fog.
I don't want to leave because I love this weather.
Rain. It is also dangerous and could bring harm.
But for me it is great in fact it is my greatest luck charm.
I love the rain like something dear to more so I never say kinda.
This weather is great down here,
I love out because it always rains in South Carolina.
A rainy day. Days like this are great.

I love the rain, so keep your opinion
Because I don't care what you say.
I don't know why I like the rain so much
Maybe it's pure love it just even fate.
Some say that a dog is a man's best friend,
But not if that dog is Slain.
Rain on me, rain rain drop.

Man V self or Man V Nature, oh boy do I love rain.
Rain is a beautiful wonder of the world,
Such an amazing sound could make a heart stop.
So many things in the world that bring pain.

I just think of the gift from God and hope that it rains.
It is just amazing and something special is sent.
Rain is great, wet, and magnificent.
Rain is like a big wet kiss from a dog.

It's the best feeling ever.
Never did like smoke nor did I like fog.
I don't want to leave because I love this weather.
Rain. It is also dangerous and could bring harm.

But for me it is great in fact it is my greatest luck charm.
I love the train like something dear to more
So I never say kinda.
This weather is great down here,
I love out because It always rains in South Carolina.

Poem for Weather

Julia Guo

Staring out the window...
Wishing the rain would go away.
Instead, it just comes down harder.
Dang.

I open the door and walk outside.
Pretty intense...
I walk back in and lightly shut the door.
The door flies back open.

Wow... Now I have to walk back and close it. AGAIN.
I hope it doesn't flood...
I hope I don't die.
I see the water leveling up.

Oh no...
How am I
going to go
to Burger King now?!

Fall?

Angela Scott

It's dark and dreary
And the leaves start to fall.
Was once hot and sunny.
Now cold and in awe.

The stars shine in these cold nights,
Making me wonder of all.
What the night sky hides,
And what lies ahead.

The new year is almost around the corner,
But not everything will change.
My morals and goals will still be the same,
To make it through this and next year.

It's dark and dreary,
And the leaves start to fall.
Was once hot and sunny.
Now cold and in awe.

Every day the Sun Shines Bright

Terry Dela Cruz

Every day the sun shines bright.
Brighter than the brightest light.
Even though it seems so clear,
It also has its darkest fear.

Now I know it's all alone,
But it's best smile is always shown.
What would happen if it was gone,
We'd never see the light of dawn.

We never cared about the sun,
We never knew how it was done.
Let's start caring about the light,
Before it goes out of sight.

Every day the sun shines bright,
Brighter than the brightest light.
Shine it in our darkest hour,
To prevail its inner power.

Every day the sun shines bright,
Especially in its darkest fights.
Every day the sun shines bright,
Brighter than the brightest light.

How?

Kenya Williams

How could smooth waves
Turn into hurricanes?
How could a beautiful ocean
Become a tsunami?
It is deep but also dark,
full of life and pain.
Tides rising
And tides falling,
Into the blue
Rough and calm.

How could tall
Strong trees
Be broken down,
And turned to something weak?
How could life soulful land
Be turned to something
Lifeless?

How could a
Sunny day turn
To a stormy night?
Clear blue skies with
Fluffy white clouds to
All grey and black,
But how?
Why?

Wisdom

Erik J. Hilden

Look I've heard echoes.
Not Neccos.
Echoes.
Snapping in the wind.
No one hears it
But me.

That's fine. I have
Time on my side.

Most days…

Feet stamping and
Positions held fast
For no good reason
Except Freedom.

It makes perfect sense.
If you are them.
Or me.
And no one has to
Understand a thing.

Why would they?
Why not stand your ground,
Grunt and growl,
Put up your dukes
And fight the good fight
Over a shirt
A hoody
Sandals
A Hair Pick
And a head band?

Why not?

The answer is not easy
To explain,
But in the mean time,
Understand.

The only way to go is forward.
All you have is the here and now.

Backward is already gone.
Swirling down the drain,
Spinning in the throne.
It is over.

And the future is undetermined.
Up for grabs.
Waiting for decisions
To be made
That are not
Unwise.

Where do you stand?
Why do you stand there?
Does it really make sense?
And is it really worth it?

And will it take you
Where you
Want
To
Go?

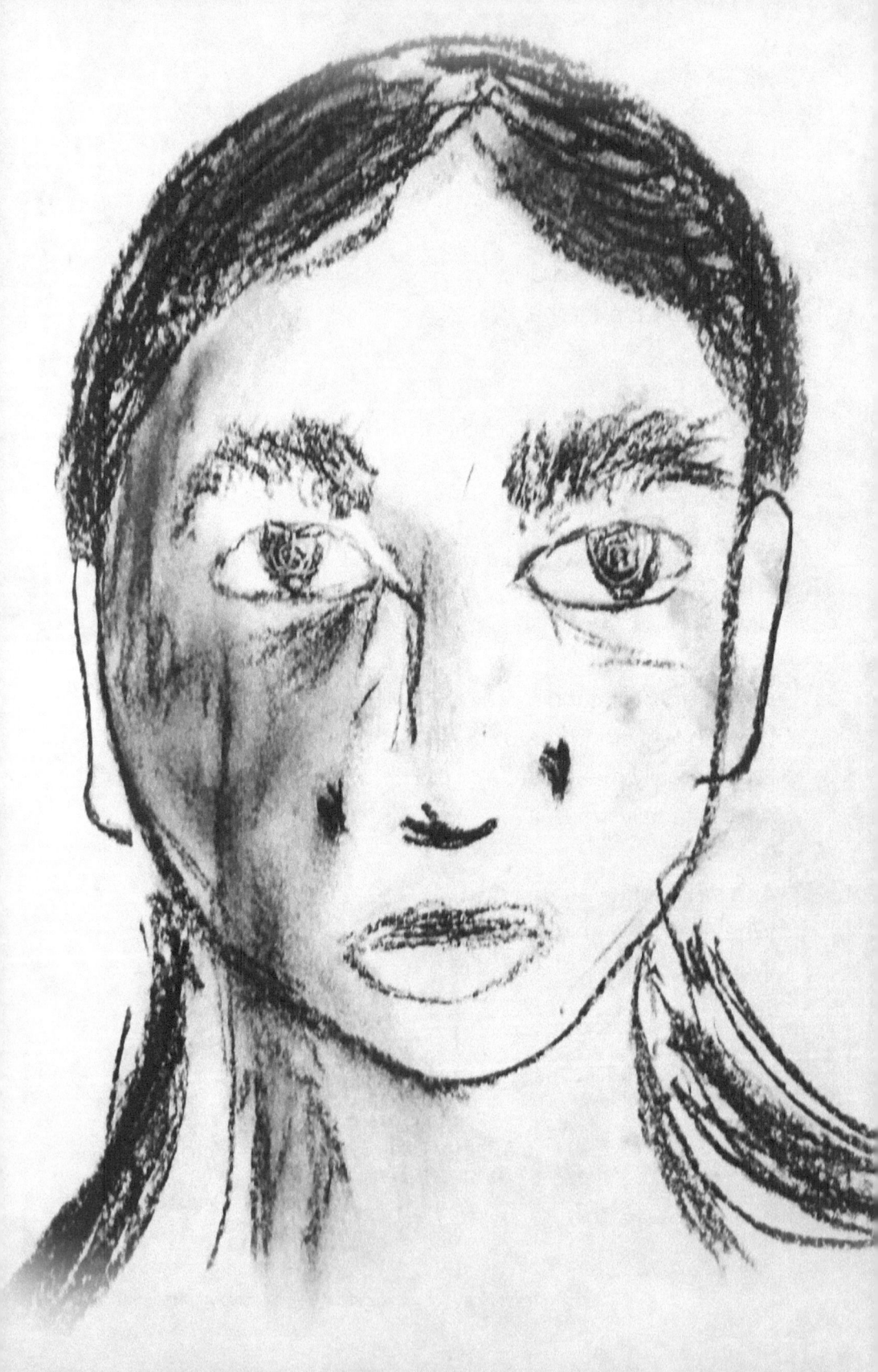

3 Love

The Rhythm

Nikki Mustipher

I fell in love with you before I met you
It was the rhythm of your heartbeat
My love for you is unfeigning
It is the rhythm of your heartbeat
Loving you is better than life it's self
It is because of the rhythm of your heartbeat
If your heart ever stops beating
My heart will lose it's rhythm
My love is syncopated by the
cadence of your heartbeat...

Lover, Not a Fighter

Wendell Varner

Love is a deep array of emotion.
It curves at every turn.
An unexplainable phenomenon,
It can never be restrained.
More like a feeling of courage.
Love is powerful and may control you.
It holds the key to your soul.
There isn't a spare.
Love is the girl you want to take to prom.
You can't find the courage.
She is like a beautiful butterfly,
So discouraged, until she flies away.

Love From Within

Angela Scott

What are you talking about? It is a sin?
No matter what I say, I can never win!
But it doesn't matter, cause I know I'm strong.
All around the world, there are people like me.

Varieties of people, all connected in a community.
Religion is against it, but you don't just choose it.
You were born this way, no need to be ashamed.
We are all the same, supported by friends.

Each and every way, and no matter what they say,
Or what they do, I'll always know in my heart
I love me, and everything I do.
Others may say the same, the others
That had the experience.

The others that have been through the joy,
The others that have been through the pain,
The others who were stuck, in between the blame game.
But they all have different ways to overcome the pain.
But it's not that simple, it never is.

But all in all, it's what on the inside that counts.
Not the appearance, or what love they have,
Because love comes in different shapes and sizes.
Cause there's nothing else that people despise,
Than not being able to love who they want.

To love, Without hate or demise.

You All Know Her Name

Kyeara Grate

Deception is her name,
She wears it well.
From her eyes to her thighs,
Could you tell?

She has deceived the nations,
Played you all like music.
If she was the composer,
You were the influence.

While the heats on for y'all,
She's keeping cool.
Teaching y'all like y'all her students,
And life is like a school.

I met her,
What a pleasure to meet.
She treated me like royalty,
From my head to my feet.

If only I hadn't,
I wouldn't have suffered the heartbreak.
For she took my love,
And left me with hate.

Love and Steam

Aydan Kapinos

When the fire stays away from the water,
The father tells his daughter.
But when the water stays away from the sun,
The mother tells his son.

When they collide, it makes steam.
Each guardian will tell them to
Redeem.

When they hide,
They have pride.
To come together as bride.
She has lied
To her father.

Same as spouse.
He's covered in douse.
He lied to his mom.
He takes her palm,
And says goodbye.

Black Queen

Kyeara Grate

Round of applause for the Queen B.
She deserves a crown,
'Cause she's a star.
Babygirl, always in my heart.

Wrote this for you,
Because you're worth it.
Made it out of the streets.
You deserve it.

Two kids, two jobs,
Made it on your own.
Independence is your name.
You deserve a throne.

Keep it pushing for the kids,
Show them that you are proud.
Everybody raise your hands,
And shout it out loud.

I'll Be The One

Kenny Coronel

If he needed someone,
Would he give me a chance?
If he needed to be loved,
Would he give me a chance?

If he needed a hug,
Would he give me chance?
If he needed a kiss,
Would he give me a chance?

If he needs someone,
I'll be the one he needs.
If he needs to be kissed,
I'll be the one he kisses.

If he needs a hug,
I'll be the one he hugs.
If he needs to be loved,
I'll be the one he loves.

You Say You Love Me

Kenny Coronel

You say you love me.
Do you seek me as blissful relief,
Or part of your list
Which surely I've missed?

Another one of your enemies,
Which of course you have plenty,
You are just doubled faced,
Easy for you to be misplaced.

You say something at first,
Then cause tears to burst.
Eyes meet each other,
Seeking for its real lover.

Another day passes by,
And you're still a dark sky,
Which has no light,
That can't shine at night.

As others find themselves,
You're still not reading a book off the shelves.
I'm here.
Then you decide to hear.

It took me a while to know me,
But it happened when I was free.
When I left you.
But who really knew?

I wanted to know,
But you wouldn't let me go.
You're not the one,
So go ahead, 'cuz I already won.

I know who I am.
Sadly you can't.
So go find another victim.
Hopefully they listen.

Friends Forever

Yahira Gonzalez

A friend is like a flower.
A rose, to be exact.
Or maybe like a brand new gate,
It always comes unlatched.

A friend is like an owl,
Both beautiful and wise.
Or perhaps a friend is like a ghost,
Whose spirit never dies.

A friend is like a heart that
Goes strong until the end.
Where would we be in this world,
If we never had a friend?

Ballet Recital

Hannah Parrish

Raindrops being pulled towards the bottom of my window.
I sit and think of you.
The fire crackling still pounding in my ears
The red and orange dancers twirl into my vision.

Your body. Your smile. My love.
My heart. Your heart. Intertwined .
I remember the recital like it was yesterday.
The red and orange ballerinas danced in perfect harmony.

Your body compressed into ashes.
My heart, along with you.
The grand finale was dark.
I tried to find you in the audience;

You were nowhere to be seen.
Was it an intermission?
No, it couldn't be.
The show was over.

The dancers took a bow.
They took you, too.
The house was torn down brick by brick.
The roof, destroyed.

Your eyes. Your smile. Your kiss.
The dancers took.
They have taken what they can't give back.

The fire burned.

I will find you.
I will find those dancers.
I will be with you again.
Once again.

Never A Fool For You

Kyeara Grate

As the walls are closing in,
I can hardly breathe.
For you've ripped my heart out of my body.
My soul's slowly letting go.

I see the white light,
Do I dare go near?
For my faith has been contradicted by sins.
I know that the end has come.

The death of me.
The end of me.
My soul is slipping away.
Why did you break my heart?

You don't seem to see,
That I am slowly fading.
For my white light has turned gray.
I am no longer alive.

I loved you.
Many times I fell for your games.
You didn't love me back.
I should've left you alone.

But like a great man said "Fool me once, shame on you"
You'll never fool me twice.
And mark my words,
For I won't give you the satisfaction of my time.

Are you jealous?
That I don't need you anymore?
You'll never again get my heart.
I will never let you into that door.

I've found someone,
He makes me happy.
He loves me-
And I love him too.

Never Again Will I Be Your Fool.

Diamonds & Rings

Samiyah Frasier

Everything was fake.
The love, the passion.
Everything was a complete lie.
I feel betrayed.

You lie, cheat, and steal.
You are worth nothing of my time.
Can I trust you?
Didn't think so.

But thats okay.
The love of my life is waiting for me
Around the corner,
So he can swoop me in his beloved arms.

Then I'll look at you,
And laugh at your pain.
The pain you caused me.
I will seek revenge.

Sooner than later,
When I have my fist.
My fist full of diamonds,
Hands full of rings.

Diamonds and Pearls

Kyeara Grate

I won't give you the satisfaction
Of another chance.
Fool me once, shame on you
Never again will I be your fool.

So manipulative,
Can't believe I fell for you.
Your love was so vain,
Your heart was immature.

I wanted something established,
You wanted something else.
Big thighs and round hips,
Will never be compromised.

I am a young woman.
I stand strong and proud.
Always a crowd pleaser,
And a head turner.

Diamonds and Pearls,
Maybe worth the world.
But one thing you'll never have
Is this girl - Ever Again.

4 Respect

What it is

Anonymous

Like, they want it... But they have no idea what it is.
Their lack of knowing can be heard in every
Curse word they utter in your presence,
Through every sucked tooth and rolled eye,
That not getting it is really not told why.

You just felt belittled by some little old guy,
Who looked you in your eye and told a bold lie.
"You don't love us!"
The words cut deeper than you thought they should.

While you contemplated doing more harm than good,
Showing him that you could actually hack it in his hood,
Only wishing that suckah really would...
So then you could really show him what it is,

And in turn show them what it is.
That it's earned and not for free,
That it's learned and not from me,
That it begins with their family, their history...

Like I said, they want it, but they have no idea what it is.
It's just a concept; a word, that keeps
bouncing off their ears,
From lips they've been taught don't actually exist.
The same lips that tell them how it really is.

The same lips that they will actuallynever really hear,
Until...
Until it becomes too late,
And they are no longer here because of their hate.

Because they only knew to imitate,
And never fully understood how to dictate
This thing they say they want.
But, they have no idea what it is.
... it's respect.

And until they know, they'll never know.

Table

Kyeara Grate

It becomes more acceptable during the holidays.
No sit at the table and eat.
Instead we turn to others...
Oh, how this is bittersweet.

The table is the church,
We're the congregation.
Like if Jesus were the law,
And we are the new nation.

We need to come together.
Build up our young men.
They need more role models,
Because the chance of survival is thin.

We need to show our young women,
How exactly to grow.
They have nothing to prove,
So why let it show?

But we can't do this,
Because we're not at the table.
Instead families are growing further apart.
Just like Cain and Abel.

Don't forget this place
That leaves nostalgia in your heart.
The place where Grandma taught you
That "This Is Where It Starts."

People Will Understand

Samiyah Frasier

He told me,
"I don't understand you."
Am I not clear enough?
Do I have to do it again?

I don't understand
How people don't understand me
In any of my perspectives.
Am I really that different?

I'm human just like the rest.
What's so hard to get is that
I hate the fact that they don't get it.
It makes me anger…shiver.

One day people will understand…
UNDERSTAND ME…just one day.
I'll be waiting for that day,
When they don't look at me differently.

Bad Girl

Julia Guo

I'm known as the "bad girl" and I don't care.
How does it hurt if all they do is stare?
I like wearing black and I like getting mad.
I think the label is cool because I'm BAD.

They don't understand I choose to live like this.
I make my own decisions, the thing they always miss.
And to prove my point that I control this madness,
I put it to the test and show them my badness.

I graffiti the school chairs with the word BAD,
I trash the hallways with all the F tests I've had.
Have I done this before or so you ask?
Only twice but the first time behind a mask.

I've been caught oh no I really hope they don't
Send me away.
Oh please I wish I could have it that way.
They're tired of my behaving and they're sick of my drama
I said they can suck it and they threatened to
Call my mama.

But I'm happy she's coming to drive me back home
Where she and I can talk all alone,
It's these times I love the most…
When a mother and daughter get more close.

I miss my mom but she's always busy.
She doesn't know my heart is missing.
Missing her, to be exact...
That is why I put on the act.

I want to spend time with her,
But she won't hear me out.
So, I couldn't handle it.
My final act was to SHOUT.

MOM COME HERE I NEED TO TELL YOU SOMETHING
IM BAD FOR ATTENTION NOT JUST FOR NOTHING
I MISS YOU VERY MUCH YOU NEVER NOTICE ME
LOOK AT ME MOM FOCUS PLEASE...

She turns her head and saids with a smile...
"Honey I love you"
"Then why do you ignore me?"
"To make you realize I've treated my mother with
that same ignoring act for most of my life.

And you are always trapped in your room
with your laptop and phone."
"Don't waste the time you have with your loved ones."
"And honey, I ignored you for one week..."

My mom was right.
I'm too dramatic!
I honestly do love her more than my phone and laptop.
I guess I'm just a love-my-mom fanatic!

I Am

Kyeara Grate

I am what you say I am.
Though you may not see,
What you say I am
Is what I'll really be.

I am disrespectful, rude,
A liar too.
Though you may not see it,
Its really coming true.

I don't like those names,
But that's what I'll be.
See, telling me these names
Doesn't just affect me.

I am becoming more distant,
Contemplating to sin.
My light is slowly fading,
From bright to dim.

I am what you say I am.
That's just how it'll be.
Do me a favor,
And set me free.

Regrets

Jesus Alarcon

Pick your shoes up, No response.
Please pick your shoes up.
Laughter, and a mocking voice.
PICK YOUR SHOES UP.

Shoe thrown across the room.
The shoe missed it's target.
Anger and annoyance filled his heart.
And the Hammurabi code in mind.

Another shoe was thrown.
But this time, it had hit its target.
The damage had been done.
Pain filled her young and weak body.

Tears of pain, and now the mother was in the room.
She demanded an explanation.
He was speechless, he was guilty, he was a coward.
Regret filled his mind, he knew the consequences.

From nowhere comes a voice, a crying voice of sympathy.
Tears in her eyes, and a smile sprouting.
She was in pain and said it was my fault I tripped and fell,
Don't blame him.
His heart was touched forever.

5 Trouble

Words

Jane'a Smith

People don't know what they say hurts.
They didn't know that their words did the work.
People say they're good and strong.
I've been there, done that, and they're wrong.

I know you're hurting from what those people said.
Why do you let it get to you?
Why do you let it in your head?
They laugh and hit you and call you all nerds.
Just try to remember all you heard were words.

These Are Only Fairytales

Hannah Garcia

Because Cinderella escaped
From her misery by a prince.
Because Aurora was awakened
From her eternal sleep by a kiss.

Because Bell had been taken
From her pathetic life by a beast.
Because these are only fairytales,
Everyone has to save themselves
From their own tragedy.

Because we're all broken records
From old cardboard boxes.
Because we're all imperfect dolls
From little mechanical machines.

Because we're all birds with broken wings
from the little nest called Heaven.
It changes from nine a.m. to nine p.m.
And I can't feel my heart beat in my chest anymore.

The Happiness Tree

Kayla Cannady

Where did you plant it?
Where did it go?
What soil is needed,
For the happiness tree to grow?

I've seen its small seed,
I have watched it barely sprout.
It did not fully develop.
Why is that so? What's that about?

To see it's entirety
And the fruit it bears,
To taste its fruit of sweet joy
Leaving me feeling like I'm walking on air.

I wish I had the chance
To plant and grow the happiness tree.
But they've killed it with a unique pesticide,
Known as the darkness in me.

The Freedom of Being Myself

Saleema El-Amin

Perhaps excluding myself from everyone helps.
I give gratifying favor to the bullies that view me as weak.
Often times I contradict myself before I even try.
Over time, I introverted.

I thought back to my past life,
however I showed no sympathy.
I am a pedagogue; viewed with high power
Their words don't seem to bother me anymore.

My old thought of being scared of pugnacious kids so faded.
My actions will not be retroactive.
I'm moving forward.
For one day I will be accepted,
And forever liberated.

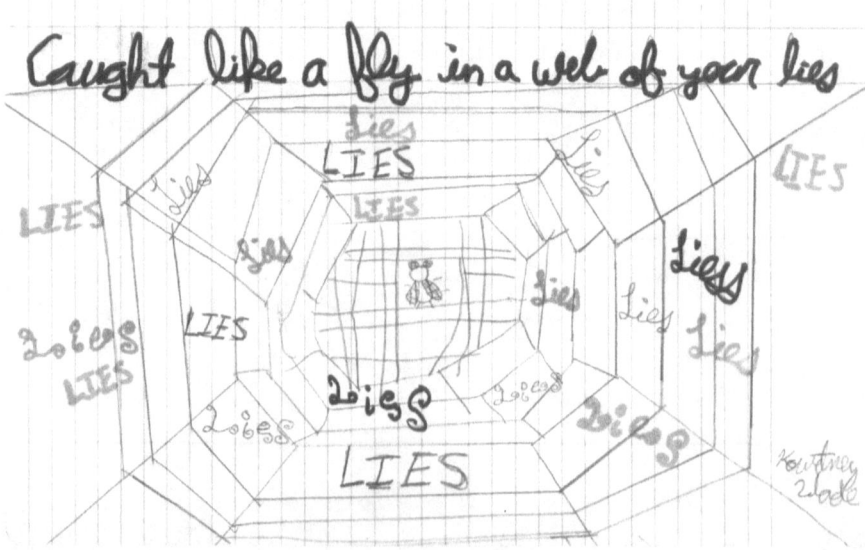

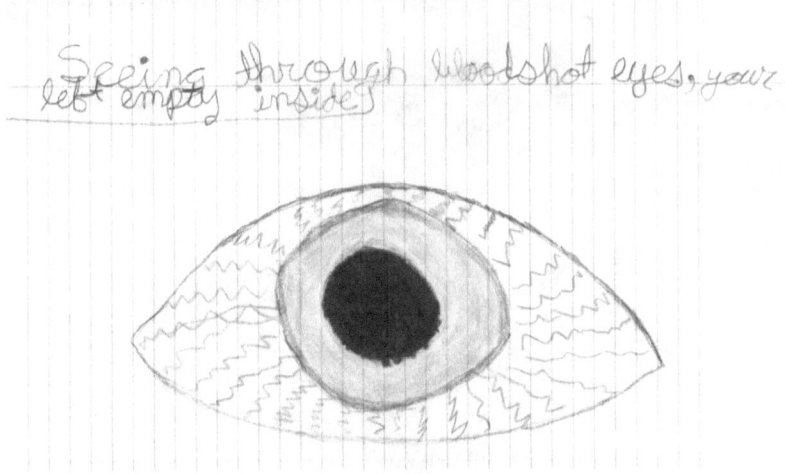

Seeing through bloodshot eyes, your
left empty inside

Molding Who I Am

Erica Stoker

YOU GRABBED MY WRIST AND LED ME HOME;
TO THE STAGE YOU BUILT IN YOUR BACK YARD
THE CURTAINS MADE OF OLD BED SHEETS
EACH NIGHT I COULD BARELY SLEEP

THE SAME OLD NINE TO FIVE TIME
SAME OLD WORTHLESS UNFUNNY LINES
YOU THREW ME UP TO YOUR WOODEN STAGE
MY WHOLE LIFE HAS BEEN A SCRIPT AND YOU WROTE
EVERY PAGE

YOU WANTED CONTROL SO I COUGHED IT UP
CHOKED ON MY WORDS, RAN OUT OF LUCK
YOU BEGAN MOLDING WHO I WAS
I KNEW FROM THE START THAT YOU WERE NOT TO TRUST

How the Paths Sway

Morgan McClure

Time withers us away,
Making it to where we can't say
What we want, til it's too late.
We have so much time,
But it always seems to slip away.

Everything is changing.
Every path is under different sway.
For some they will never see the light of day.
For some that's all they see anyway,
And some it's just pure grey.

But as we wither away,
We change the way our path sway.
From black to grey,
From grey to white,
It truly changes our sight.

Because what we see
Is based on what we believe,
And that's what makes our paths change,
From insane to sane and the other way.
That's how our paths sway.

Missing

Trey Hensley

Sometimes—we feel a part of us, missing, absent, misplaced.
What is it that's missing?
It could be the part that makes you happy.
It could also be the part, that makes up you.

No matter—what you're missing,
Something else can replace that missing piece.
It can make you feel better,
It may redefine you.

Life can always have missing pieces,
But, when that replacement comes,
Don't be afraid to talk. Don't be afraid to open up.
Be open because that person, can replace that missing piece.
That "special replacement."

That "special replacement" can be the person,
You cherish forever.
Your soul mate.
Developing the "missing" feeling, can lead to wonderful things—
In your life.

That missing piece,
Will soon be filled,
With your new piece.
Your "special replacement."

Losers

Harvey Hamilton

Broken locks and broken windows.
Having no regrets, until a shot is fired.
The cops killed the wrong man.
Everything is gone .
Nothing but trash.
Stains of your past,
All over the ground.
The villains just
Laugh…
Laugh…
Laugh…
Dead in the street.
Innocent blood spilled.
As the villains laugh,
The people weep.
The different races,
Blacks and Mexicans,
Mad because of their rights being bothered.
Mad because they broke the trust.
Now they made us LOSERS.

Change of Heart

Julia Guo ·

As I sit here, tortured
That people might think ridiculous,
I am sophisticated,
Incapable of being ridiculed.

Your spirit will not haunt me.
Separated from others who are stupidly
Into your pit of blind happiness,
I stand solid but then...

Horrified, petrified...
In this confusion I realized,
Well, to be brief, I myself fell, as well.
Inspired by this sudden change,

I start to think, philosophy.
You, the culprit, I, the victim
But you lie there so amiable,
Of all the basic colors.

I now start to think you are the ultraviolet.
Has it ever occurred to you
That you are the beauty?
And I sigh. I am merely a plain pattern.

Breaking Down

Samiyah Frasier

Drip...Drop...Drip...Drop I looked out the window,
Watching the rain fall as the tears began
To run down my face.
What is wrong with me?
I forgot everything is wrong with me...
Why is hatred upon me?
I may not know until someone tells me right?

I feel depressed about my life...
Does society really hate me?
Yes...no...I don't know.
Nothing is the same. I'm not the same
Happy little girl I once was.
Happy, enjoyment, excitement, that I was once filled with.
Now its slowly fading away.

I feel depression, aggression, and...empty.
Again, I ask what is wrong with me?
Yet I still don't have answers.
I am now coming to the realization. Not only am I sad.

I am physically .....Breaking Down.

An Educated Woman

Tilayah Bennett

She may have her ups and downs and her flaws.
She may cry through her pain and lies all night long.
And be around all the negativity that she sees.
But she is still an educated woman.

There might be clouds blocking her way.
But she will still smile and brightens your day
She may laugh through her emotion but...
She still is an educated woman at the end of the day.

It's good to have a woman who knows her stuff.
Treat her right, and she'll stick around long enough.
Just remember, an educated woman
Is a good woman, indeed

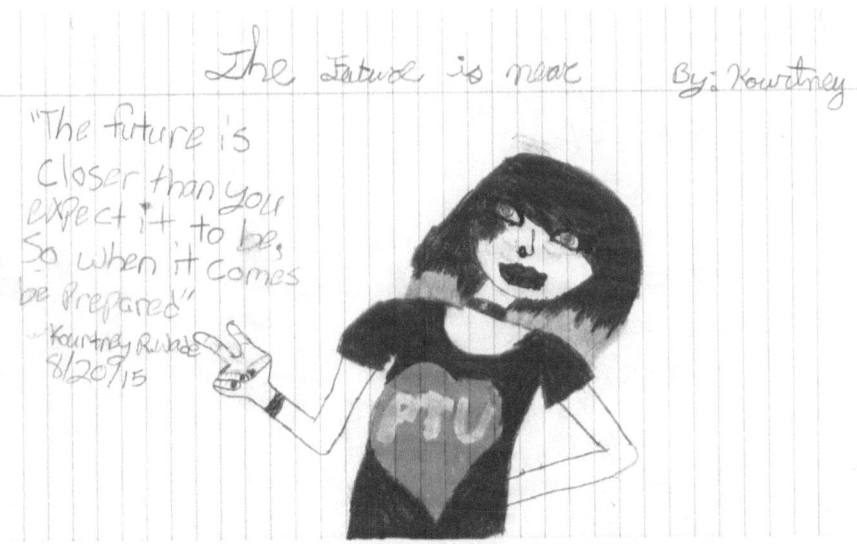

The future is near   By: Kourtney

"The future is
closer than you
expect it to be,
so when it comes
be prepared"
— Kourtney Rivas
8/20/15

Never, Will You Know

Jalynn Henryhand

Dark as night I see my soul,
For the forbidden
Has been done.
Tears in the inside,
Hollow and broken,
Wishes for acceptance,
Only to be hurt over
And over again.
No one understands.
Different, out of gravity,
Forever alone in the pits of darkness.
Built walls.
Dangerous,
Evil,
Mean walls.
Only a few see the cracks.
Tiny things
You will never break.
You can only destroy.
Yet, no
Spirits.
I trust NO ONE.
They are all specks of life.
People who want to kill,
Not glass,
Not sunshine.

Oh so far am I from
So you won't see me.
Not unless i open up the gates of pain.
Hide so well,
Yet they ask 'what's wrong?'
You will, they will, we will
Never ever know.

Why?

Angela Scott

Everything was good.
There was nothing to fear.
Just the two of us together,
Swinging soundly on our secret swing.

But then they found out.
They took everything away.
The one that I loved,
The one who said It'll be okay.

But it's been so long,
My worries unsettling,
Images running through my head,
The fear trembling.

But one day, it happened so suddenly.
My phone sang abruptly.
I swiftly answer it, my heart crumbling,
".. I'm sorry.."

Thoughts

Kyla Wright

As though the cat caught my tongue,
I don't make a sound.
I back away from your compliments
As my lips try to open, but I am still silent.
Staring at the wall, daydreaming,
I just have to think of something,
but what can I say?
Thoughts running and playing in my head.
Just cannot find its way to come out.
I just want to say hi,
But I am misleading, and it came out as bye.
I try to make myself an acquaintance.
My mind just told me to keep my distance.
I need to learn to get comfortable.
Express myself.
Not just on the inside,
But the outside.
I just want to come out and say hello.
Open the doors to an amazing conversation.
But what if I say the wrong thing?
I will be embarrassed, crushed, and broken.
I dare myself to slowly separate my lips
And make a sound.
No longer am I afraid, because this is life.
My inner self has been found.
Communication is the key.
Communication helps you learn.

Communication helps you thrive.
Communication helps the world.
Only if you know what is right.
Shy to Outspoken,
Quiet to Vociferous,
Dull to Lively,
My voice is my power.

I was wrongfully accused, you left my locked inside a cell

Poem for loss

Julia Guo

It's gone…
Forever.
In the deep, dark, bitter hole,
There it lies.
Crying.
Screaming for help.
It wants out.
But there is no way out.
It is locked in a box.
A box filled with other trapped prisoners.
There it sees…
Trust, love, and happiness.
They tell Soul they will be in the box for all of eternity.

Pressure

Ca'Shun Barr

Studying hard every night,
Trying to be me.
Trying to beat him,
Over, and over again.
Trying to get her but she keeps running,
Running forever it seems,
And I'm finally caught up,
In the lead forever.
But it doesn't feel good.
My love for her was stronger than my love for the win.
Gears turning in my head,
So I don't get ahead.
Outpost beat.
Trying to be free, of all of this work, I'm stuck,
And I'm drowning in this pile of papers.

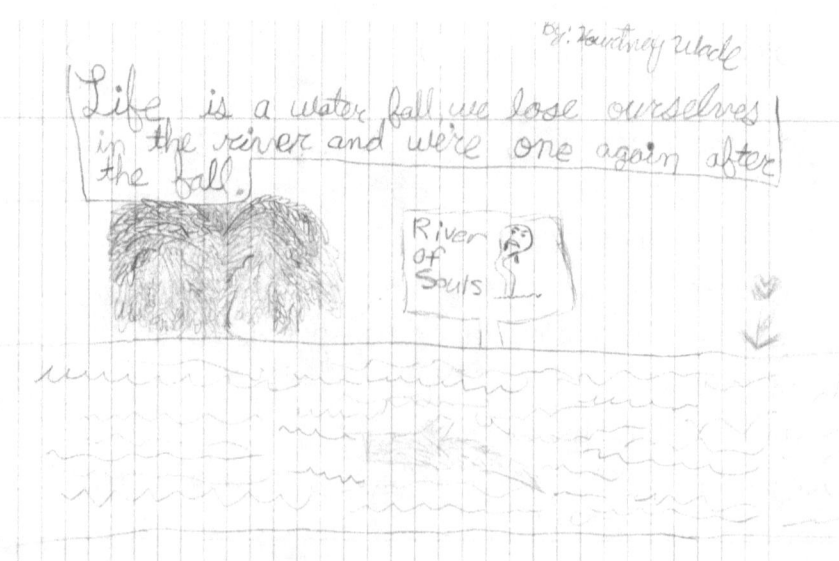

Another day in Mexico

Daniel Hernandez

Mothers weeping, guns speaking,
Drugs are ruling, police shooting.
This is just another day in Mexico.

Another day with violence and coke.
The narcos are taking over,
With cocaine coming from Colombia
And AK's from Russia.

But what the government doing?
Why are the people booing?

I see blood on the street.
I see the bodies piled on the cold concrete.
I see my peoples' face full of tears,
Sobbing about dead friends and peers.

Cartels, shootings, and drive-bys.
The daily routine of a Mexican's life.
Always worrying about getting killed.
Hoping their "worry" is not fulfilled.

6 Growing Up Dreaming

What If You Believed?

Jemiell Laguitao

I've always wondered things, I'm not sure why
I'm always thinking, I'm always dreaming,
Never once have I thought too little
about something to abide by,
So what if I started with a what if?

What if I wasn't placed onto this earth?
What if I wasn't born?
What if I said I wanted to go?
What if I said I needed to go?

It doesn't matter if I think I should go.
It doesn't matter when.
I'm living, aren't I? So let me.
Set me free, I'm on my way.

What if I had an adventure?
What if I just left you behind?
What if you missed me?
What if I didn't really care?

Would you follow me,
Or would you wait?
Would you remember me,
Or would you forget?

What if I could fly?
What if I could soar with the wind?
What if the stars guided me?
What if a cloud took me away?

What if the sky wasn't blue?
What if the moon wasn't there to shine our night?
What if the trees weren't green?
What if the sea wasn't so deep?

What if there's another world out there?
What if there's life on another planet?
What if there's something much bigger than us?
Yet what if there's something smaller than us?

What if I had a twin?
What if you couldn't tell a difference?
What if I wasn't your friend?
What if I wasn't family?

What if I was rich?
What if I was poor?
What if you loved me?
What if you hated me?

What if things were to happen?
What if I were there?
What if I wasn't?
What if you acted different?

What if I watched you?
What if I understood you?
What if I thought of you?
What if I learned from you?

What if I could dream?
What if I could believe?
What if you trusted me?
What if you believed?

When I Was Little

Devonte Alston

When I was little,
I used to have dreams
That the people from before
Would be
In the same place as me.

All of these dreams
Are now leaving me.
Slowly,
But surely.

But almost as quickly,
As my promises and dreams,
My options and pleads,
All turned into a ball of smoke.

Slowly,
But surely,
I lay awake,
And listen to paper planes
As I cry and reminisce
About the happy past,
And about all of the friends that I used to have.

I now realize that remembering is not enough.

I have to actually find what I want to do
With my life and go through with it,
Before I go around chasing the friends
That I used to want to stick with.

I'm losing friends and acquaintances,
And just waiting to see how their lives all switch.
I sit and remember all the times I use to enjoy
And sit and shed tears of sorrow and joy,

And just wish
That if they leave,
I'll cross paths with all of them again.

Will they all be different,
Or will I be the same?
Life for all of us,
A mystery it will remain.

Do It

Quinton Adams

When we are here,
When we are done,
We all will shout with great cheer,
Once passed has become time,
It will then be our time to shine.

We will overcome and work as a team,
Once we are finished we all can dream
Of things that we did,
When we all were kids.

Once upon a time,
We will shine,
Once we finished and are all done,
As a group we all will overcome.

Dear No One

Jasmain Jenkins

Dear No One...
I answer the phone.
To hear nothing on the other end
No laughing. No Talking. No Nothing.
Nowhere to begin.
I start to daydream about the things we could do.
Then I realize with
WHOM DO I DO?
Sometimes I try to imagine who you could be,
But I always end up blinded
by who I picture & want to see.
When all I have to do is OPEN MY EYES & SEE.
Because you were always right there,
Standing next to me.
Maybe its that 'Coming Of Age' experience I once
Wished to conceive.
But now since it's here, I wish it would leave me BE.
And still I write this poem that
Only I may understand and see.
But before I try to find you I need to FIND ME.
I need to get up and search for you,
Before someone else finds you.
OR I could do nothing.
And you will remain
Dear No One to me.

Desire

Samiyah Frasier

People have so many desires
That desire can drive you crazy.
Are you willing to still have your desire?
Are you willing to do anything?

I am a fourteen year old girl
With a desire,
And it makes me angry that I can't have it,
That I can't stand for what I believe in.

I can't change their minds at all.
That is why I am what I am today.
That's why I will never change.
I can't go back to the way it use to be.

I'm never gonna change.
Because of them…
I crave that my desire comes true.
My desire to be free.

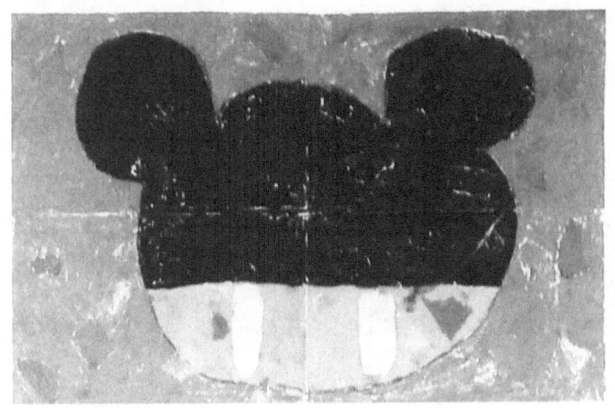

What Is?

Matthew White

What is life?
Is it real?
Or are we puppets on a stage?
It's full of strife
On this journey we call life.

What is love?
Is it supposed to fit like a glove?
Is it fair?
All it does is make you wash your hair.

What is fear?
Isn't it just an evil glare?
Isn't it just luring your mind
Out of your head? Out of your ear?
So don't you fear.
I am here!

What Lies Underneath

Syncere Washington

They said we'd be okay,
But what they didn't understand
Is that now a beautiful diamond
That was once just a handful of sand.

Under everyone's smiles can lie
Torment, torture, and demand.
Behind the blue skies
Are gray clouds ready to make amends.

What we need is kindness,
But instead they are mean.
They suffer from blindness.
Forgiveness is power.

Make your hatred blossom,
Because what lies underneath can be a
Beautiful
Flower.

Practice

Leticia Velasco

She kicked the ball and it hit his face.
When she tried out she came in last place.
He wanted her off the team right away.
But she was pleased and pleased to stay.
He rolled his eyes and let out a sigh.
She said why can't I play like those guys.

Days and days past and she was still bad.
He got angrier each day and was mad.
Months of practice and even more.
She didn't even care if she was sore.

He saw the improvement in her skills.
He also saw her mess ups and fails.
He'd thought she stayed the same.
They got to the field and saw everyone stare.

He was confident but she was scared.
Days away were their big game.
She was good, even the best.
But he was just a mess.

She looked at him and smiled.
And he looked at her and smiled.

American Dream

Daniel Hernandez

When my mom and dad crossed the border,
They wanted to go "North,"
Where they would get more money
And better support.

Back in Mexico, my family used to say,
"The North is the American Dream."
Ha, must have been a joke,
Because when my parents got here,
They were discriminated against.
They were Mexican folks.
My parents were made fun of.
Wetbacks, aliens, beaners.

I just wanna cry when I hear this.
I feel bad for my parents.
I just want them to forgive my stupid mistakes.
I just want to-
Give them a big kiss.

My Thoughts Aren't The Same

Jalynn Henryhand

See equanimity.
Stay sediment.
Go through that metamorphosis.
Jumble up the miracle
In between that fort.
Reify that choice.
Your sooooo sure.
Dynamically confident.
WAIT…no
Voice.

Go beyond your regular thoughts.
Switch it up.
I automatically...
I can see the picture, now.
Blind, I can see…it's this.
Take the chance.
Pick up your pen.

Predict.

Is what I am seeing really my choice?

Life

Ca'shun Barr

Scary, beautiful, exciting, fearful,
We all try to live life to the fullest,
To fulfil our destiny.
Step outside the box, become a millionaire.

Anything is possible.
Don't let fear stop you, stand up for those who can't
Stand up for themselves.
The fear of never knowing what's next.

Just remember, nothing lasts forever.
You'll wake up and realize it's all over.
Because we all need a little help, sometimes.
Enjoy life down to the very last breath,

And never give up.

Eternal Dream

Samiyah Frasier

Me in my own world.
It's satisfaction to me.
All the imagery
Is mine and only mine.

Me being able to lay down,
And fall into my eternal dream,
Brings me happiness.
It brings me life.

In my eternal dream,
It is finally giving me peace…
That freedom I've always wanted.
I feel relieved.

No screams, no cries, no stress,
Finally thinking for myself.
No one is telling me what to say.
No one is telling me what to do.

I am my own control.
My thoughts finally matter.
Someone cares in my dreams.
Just not in reality.

The Light

Jamel Cunningham

The light...it was a bright light.
I went to that bright light.

It was so beautiful.
I heard music playing.
Angels singing.

But it was not my time.
The light fades away.
The light was gone.

Everything was black.
I was scared.
I wish that light was not gone.
I wanted someone to stay with me.

I woke up from that dream.
I had my loved ones with me.
My class, I know, they will take care of me,
And will not let anybody hurt me.

I never dreamed
About that light again.
I am going to live
My life
In peace.

Nathaniel Flowers

A graphic novel by Tekaysha T. Hagler

At a young age, he witnessed the U.S. soldiers training for war.
It inspired him so much that he wanted to become one.
"I really want to become one of those soldiers."

Refusal of the call

When he graduated high school he decided that he was joining the military instead of college, but he didn't know what decision he was making. He talked to his mother before the call, she said... "I want you to think about this alright. I'm not saying "No", I'm just telling you to think about this. If you want to do it I will respect your decision and if you don't want to do this, I still will respect your decision, but just think about this, oh baby." "Yes mam. Yes mam, I will"

The beginning of the adventure

Instead of just going there, he waited. He waited until he finished college to join the military. He told his mother and she thought the same. She was relieved that her son waited a little longer to join. After graduation he called the general. After their talk, he told his family about it again and the said the things they said before. His mother said "Please be careful out there and set your mind to what is right" "Yes mam"

When he went to the military, he did terrible. he failed every course because he had no military experience. The general was a little mad because he failed every course and he was so scrany. every weight he lifted, he dropped. every running course he did, he only lasted a minute and every climbing course he did, he fell.

The Road of trails

When he went to the military, he did terribly. He failed every course because he has no military experience. The general was a little mad because he failed every course and he was so scary. Every weight he lifted, he dropped. Every running course he did, he only lasted a minute and every climbing course he did, he fell.

At first he was going to give up completely, until he met Sherry. She was the lady who would always come by to visit the general, which was her father. He would always stare at her when she walks by. She was the most beautiful girl to him. One day she was trying to impress her by how string he is but still she gasped ..."are you ok?" she said. "Yes, I'm fine" he said. "It's just I can't do this. Every course I do, I fail it" said Nathaniel. "Stop right there, you're not a failure, you're just not trying hard enough. Just try harder. ok?" said Sherry. Thank you, I really needed that" he said. "You're welcome" she said. They hugged and went on about their business.

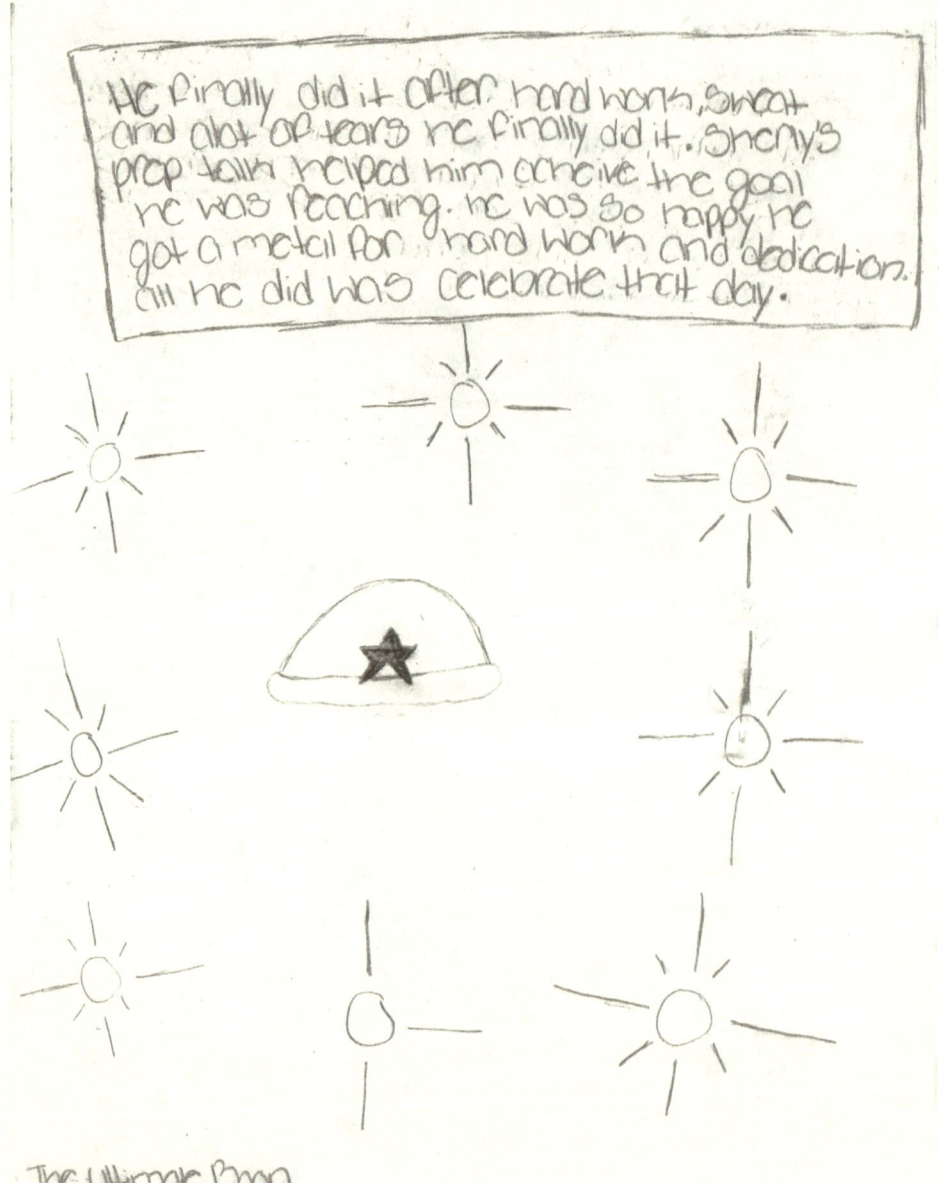

The ultimate Boon

He finally did it. After hard work, sweat and a lot of tears, he finally did it. Sherry's pep talk helped in achieve the gaol he was reaching. He was so happy he got a medal for hard work and dedication. All he did was celebrate that day.

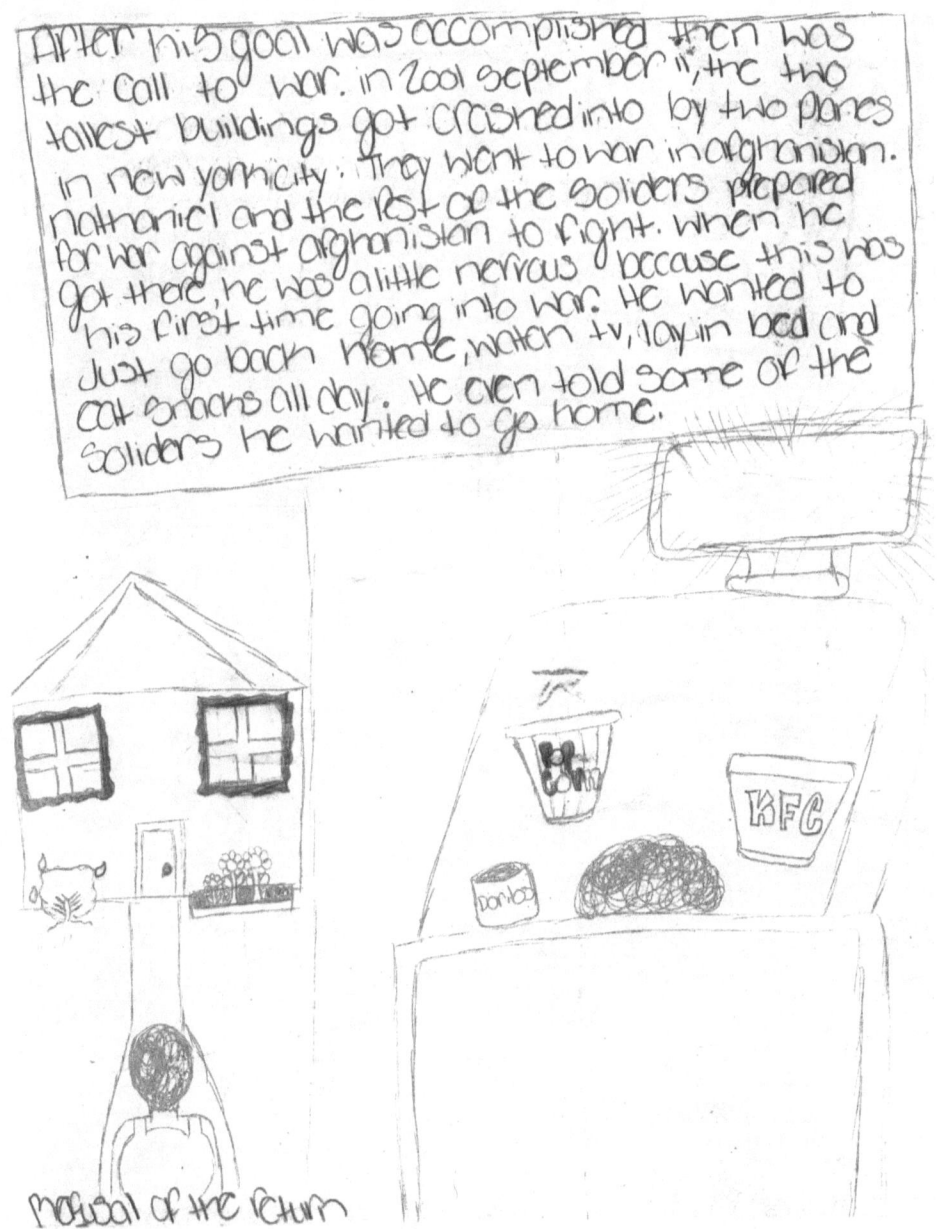

After his goal was accomplished, then he got the call to war. In 2001 September 11th, the two tallest buildings got crashed into by two planes in New York City. They went to war in Afghanistan. Nathaniel and the rest of the soldiers prepared for ware against Afghanistan. When he got their he was a little nervous because this was the first time going to war. He wanted to just go back home, watch TV, lay in bed and eat snacks all day. He even told some of the soldiers that he wanted to go home.

After all that mishap, he just realized that this is real and something you can't just get out of. He though about that going home the day after the war and everyday of his life, but if it wasn't for his families support and Sherry's advice he wouldn't have become the brave solider he is today.

The Crossing or Return Threshold

He realized that he was doing something right when the families from 9/11 thanked him for being a brave soldier and fighting for them, but all he said was.. "You don't have to thank me, I always wanted to do this as a kid."

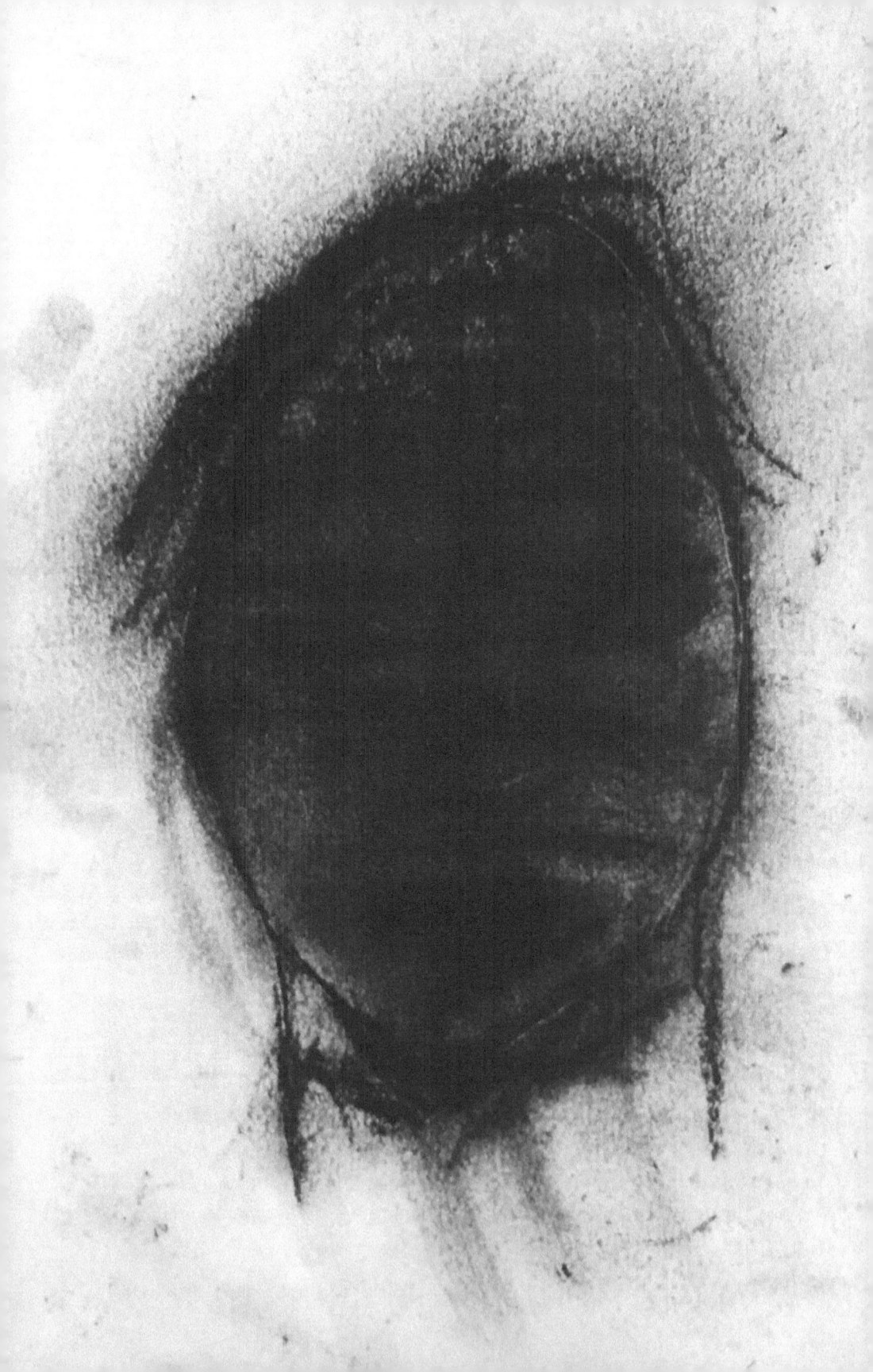

7 On Death

It Is Coming

Tristan Fryer

It is coming,
It is coming,
It will be here soon,
Never to leave,
Always there,
Just around the corner,
But gone when you get there,

Behind,
In front,
To the left,
To the right,
With you at all times,
Never leaving your side,
You did it,
You didn't,
But it's there.
Always there.

So Long

Angela Scott

It's been too long.
It seems I've forgotten your face.
What's your name again?
Why are we in this place?

The walls are white.
This space is empty.
Why aren't you saying anything?
This silence is deadly.

There is a ringing in my ear.
Can you stop it for me?
It's getting louder.
Please help me…

It's been too long.
It seems I've forgotten your face
What's your name again?
I remember now…
The forgotten face
Of my past disgrace…

The End

Samiyah Fraiser

I look outside my window.
I see nothing but thin air.
Is this how my life is going to end?
They were so many thing's I wanted to do.

I begin to cry out my sad sorrow,
As I see everything disappear,
Why must this happen to me?
To us… What went wrong?

We may never until we're nothing.
Nothing but thin air.
Slowly drifting away,
Second by second.

My cries turn into screams
As I slowly fall apart.
This is actually happening.
We are going to die.

Why? Still no answers.
Waiting and waiting and waiting.
No answer….Silence fill the room.
I blink one last time into….darkness.

Dead

Kyeara-Nyjae Grate

Dear Angel, It's your friend, Renee.
Remember...I died last May?
It was crazy to me,
How ghastly it cost.

Didn't even know that my life was lost.
But I arrived at a place.
White and Pure,
It was a beautiful sight to see.

Nothing but light, I was sure.
There was a throne, great and clean.
The man sitting, couldn't be mean.
"Renee Michelle, step forward for your time has come,"
He called out to me.

This wasn't exactly my cup of tea.
Rewinding my life,
Persecuting me.
Why couldn't I just be alone,
Put my life in the hands of one of the clones?

Then I realized I was doomed,
This was it for me.
Because I wasn't a believer,
I knew where I was going to be.

I cried out for a second chance.
He turned away every time,

For I know that He is your God.
I wish I would've made Him mine.

Now you're probably wondering,
"Where does this end?"
Just to let you know,
I'm living in a Hell hot den.

The hottest I'd ever been in my life,
Not to mention the torment,
Day and Night.
Why didn't you warn me that this is where I'll end?

Surely you must've forgot,
That my fate was sealed by the clock.
I'm in a hell, burning as wood,
While you're out laughing in the neighborhood.

You were my best friend.
How dare you not tell me?
All that time,
You didn't help me.

It's too late now.
I don't need your apologies.
For now I'm stuck,
Wishing for a hall of freedom.

By the way, I miss you much.
Just remember my softened touch.
Been quite a long time since last May.
Just wish you were here to play.

The Assassin

Samiyah Frasier

She pushed me.
I pushed back.
She pushed me.
I stabbed her.

I'm on my knees
With a wet towel,
Scrubbing the blood off the tub.
Nervousness is consuming my body.

I did what I had to do.
But was it really worth it?
Was it worth saving the ones I love?
Is it?

My first time ever in life,
I murdered someone.
I felt satisfaction, yet so anxious.

I stood on my feet and called myself
The Assassin.

Is Life Worth Living?

Jasmain Jenkins

Is life worth living?
Is my heart worth forgiving?
Is my mind too high in the sky?
Do some people get too high?

Does school make us smarter?
Does college proclaim we are stronger?
Are we truly what make society
Or is the government trying to hide?

Are we still a free country?
Because last time I checked we still follow the
Bill Of Rights!
Should we take a stand, man to man,
And settle the differences that are at hand?

Maybe we should do nothing-
And remain the same.
But that would get nothing done.
So, right now, this very day -
Get up and do something that will encourage society
In every way.

Hello And Goodbye

Leticia Velasco

The moments with them were unforgettable.
The memories were the best.
Everyday was an adventure.
The seconds we all spent were amazing.

Everyday and every night is hard without them here.
We were In each other arms.
Then he's gone.... Forever.
Everyday with him was precious.

They were hurt without him here,
So they moved away,
Far away from the pain.
No more moments with them.

No more memories with them.
No more adventures with them.
They were like the earth,
And he was like the oxygen.

No, it's over.
I can't live without the earth and oxygen.
I love them.

Falling without Gravity

Caelyn Rasmussen

Falling,falling evermore,
Never reaching ground.
Drifting closer,
Then shot back up again.

Compression on my chest,
Running out of air.

Slowly dying,
Breathless,
Full of despair.

All my friends
Have died,
So why not I?

Falling, falling evermore
Never going home,
Time to say goodbye.
Gravity has failed me.

Sinner

Samiyah Frasier

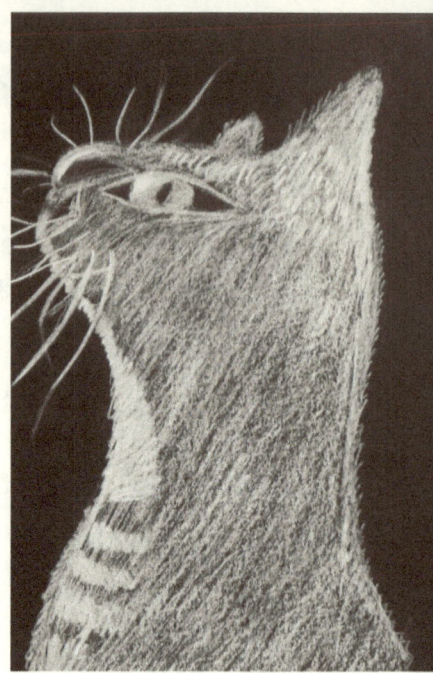

Instead of praying for God,
I'm praying for something else,
Like that is my worshipee.
Where did this come from?

I know I made a lot of mistakes,
But I didn't know
That I would end up in Hell for it,
Where everything is burning.

I looked on the other side.
There goes my family.
I slowly walk to them...I can see them.
Why can't I get over there?

I notice a glass wall.
I tapped on it...no shatters.
I knew I was the walking dead.
I knew I was the Sinner.

Oh Mama

Alyssa Kapinos

Mama, you left too early.
Auntie told me "You have to get over it, girly."
Your ship had sunk before your voyage was complete.
I miss holding your hand while walking down the street.

Oh mama, Oh mama,
I miss you badly.
Oh mama, Oh mama,
I need you madly.

Why did you have to leave
And leave me with all of this grief?
Why did you have to go
And leave me all alone?

Oh mama, Oh mama,
All of this change I cannot take.
Oh mama, Oh mama,
All of this depressing news, I have to ache.

And now I lay awake,
And wait for your return.

When You Are Gone

Kiara Brown

Please don't leave.
When you are gone,
I can't breath.

You, the air that keeps me alive.
When you are gone,
I scream for you.

As I fall on the floor,
I see you, but you're not there.

Tears fall from my face.
My face gets pale.
I try so hard to breathe,
But it's not working.

Now I see myself.
I see you come in the room,
But you're late.

I see you hold me in your arms,
Saying come back to me,
As an angel comes to get me.
It feels like I still can't breathe.

Stronger

Devonte Alston

Every day,
I come across the same bush on my way home.
For the past decade,
It's always sitting there,
Solid and still,
Being beaten and bruised by the wind.
Being deprived of its stringent leaves and
It's symmetrical figure.

And then the hurricanes strike to put it out of its misery.
It decomposes into the earth,
And circumnavigates through time.

But now,
It's been revived and has evolved
To become a more sophisticated life form.

Finally,
Ready to rebel.
Ready to rebel against the hurricanes,
With its sharp thorns,
And long arms.

It is ready
To face the world.

Gone

Jemiell Laguitao

You've been looking for a way out,
Always running around with your head down.
But now you walk the line on the high ground.
Your pride deep in the ground and now in the clouds.

At night, when the clouds fade away,
I would stare up and just look at you.
I would then look down at my hands,
Where yours fit perfectly.

And I would just think of only you and me.
I would remember the last kiss on the tips of your lips,
As well as every curve of your body,
And every shake of your hips.

I would remember the memories
Me and you once shared,
And the times you hid in my arms,
Because you were scared.

It's you that I wanted to follow,
But now you're gone.
My mind is full of sorrow.

I just watched you lay on the bed,
I saw the bloodstains on the blankets,
And you, now—are dead.

Soul to take

Samiyah Frasier

My soul isn't something to keep.
It's no good anymore.
There are no lies to tell.
There are no secrets to keep.

Beneath this something
Is something so drastic
That people will one day see.

And when that day comes
Who will be prepared for it?
Do you plan on running?
Or stay when they start …
Chasing me down.

Will you help me?
When they start pushing me to the ground,
Kicking and punching,
Pulling out the sharp butcher knife.

Grabbing my hair,
Snapping my neck,
Laying me down,
Taking my soul.

The End of Me

Kyeara Grate

As I fell to Earth,
I didn't know what I was doing.
If life was the drink,
I was drinking the fluids.

Lately I've been thinking,
"What happened to us?"
Were we weary with a burden
Or compromised by lust?

I loved you like a song,
A song I loved to sing.
You filled my heart with fire,
Like an oven it went "Bing."

Now the time has come,
My army has risen.
We're not driven by money,
But we're blood driven.

My thirst for blood,
Grows every single day.
Almost like Leonidas in Thermopylae.
Or maybe like a single flower drinking up in May.

Listen to me,
Hear my cry.

For the night has come
For me to die.

Persecute me!
Relive my sins.
For once more I tell you,
This Is The End.

Finally One Has Come

Zamani Lyde

Oh, there goes another one, we think.
With every blast of a gun,
We forget about the past,
And what we have been able to surpass.
Another son has fallen.
But will we still rise together?

And strive together?
Although we've lost another part of us,
We are still able to unite to create one,
No matter the color of your skin.

Every voice comes from within.
So will you allow your voice to be heard?
While another part of us has died,
Together we can become one and fortify.

Don't forget these words

Kyeara-Nyjae Grate

Everyday is something fresh for me,
People keep thinkin' they stressin me,
But I pay em no mind.
For one, I've got time.

You talking struggle.
Boy you blessed.
Haven't even seen the slash
Against yo mama chest.

Think you 'bout that life,
Lemme see where you stand.
We don't talk with guns.
Lemme see dem hands.

Ain't touched a tree in ya life,
Steady talking bout dope dealing is right.
Don't get yourself into no mess,
They may look like they engaged,
But they ain't 'pressed.

Why are you lying about the game?
First rule you done broke.
If you was really 'bout it,
You'd be nothing but a joke.

They got eyes and ears everywhere,
Oh you didn't know?
Just last night they been talking bout
Letting some people go.

Worried bout what's happenin in the streets,
Boy you better worry bout your life,
For God ain't promise us,
But so much time.

Make your mama proud,
She knew you had it.
Walkin across that stage,
I know you almost grabbed it.

Instead, you can't resist,
They sorry dope dealin life.

Smuggling on the streets,
You know it ain't right.

Mama sitting at the table cryin',
Boy, what'd you do?
She cryin cause somebody just took
The life of her little boo.

Don't worry though,
Cause as long as you makin dough,
You disregard yo mama feelings.

Feeling good on the outside,
But hell on the inside,
You don't know what to do.

You got the latest shoes, clothes,
All the modern trends,
But did you help your mama meet ends?

Better learn to cherish what you got,
Cause nothing lasts forever.
Friends may fade away,
But God and family are forever.

Remember these words,
Cause I promise they'll come back to you.
Don't forget the lady,
Who helped you learn how to tie yo shoe.

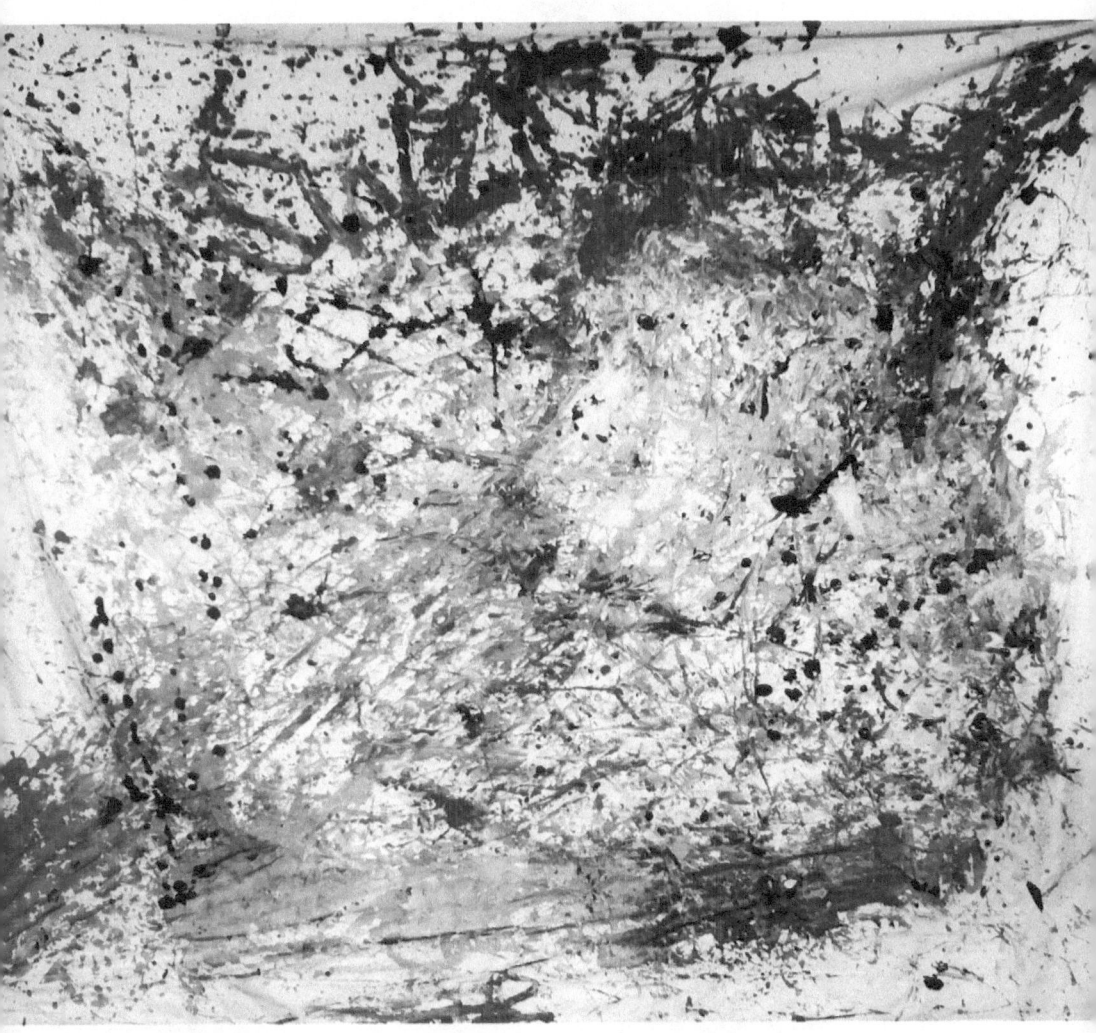

8 School Issues

Cause I Ain't Got A Pencil

Joshua T. Dickerson

I woke myself up
Because we ain't got a alarm clock.
Dug in the dirty clothes basket
Cause ain't nobody washed my uniform.
Brushed my hair and teeth in the dark
Cause the lights ain't on.
Even got my baby sister ready
Cause mama wasn't home.
Got us both to school on time,
To eat us a good breakfast.
Then when I got to class
The teacher fussed at me
Cause I ain't got a pencil.

UGH, SCHOOL

Jalynn Henryhand

Chatter. chatter. chatter.
Walk faster, ugh.
Click. click. click.
The assistant principal.

Bing. bing. bing.
Now I'm late for class.
For the box.
One teacher, 500 rules.

A pass.
You may not enter without
My record?
Stained.

Ugh, if only.
If only
Those kids would walk…
Faster.

Move around?
Blocked…again.
Get out early?
Teacher dismisses.

High school?
Can't wait.
Grades?
Stable…Ice.

New Quarter?
Another level.
Series 8, level 2.
Winning?

I don't know.
Maybe I'm not.
Failure.
Lazy.

I should make it.
America made it,
I'm not America…
I'm just…me.

Dust,
A speckle of the…
Dirt.
I will get past.

Pass the footsteps.
Pass the rules.
Pass the assistant principal.
I'm my own person.

Bing. Bing. Bing.
Made it…
Just on time.
Ugh, homework.

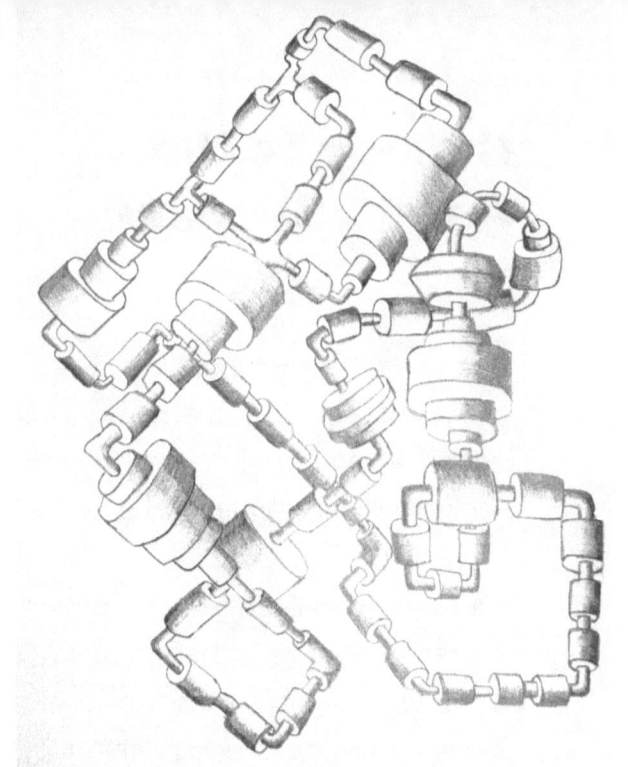

College is the Key to Success

Patrick Myers

School isn't somewhere where everyone wants to go.
We benefit from it in many ways we don't understand.
Even if we are arguing or trying to take a stand,
School will evolve you into a better man.

We all go to college to get a better knowledge.
Sometimes we're scared to ask questions
When we don't have the feel of protection,
But somehow we keep pushing in the right direction.

When you arrive at college, you have to adjust.
Sharing the restroom with 20 other guys will create a mess.
Having no one to support you will make you upset.
You just feel like quitting, I bet.

Sometimes you have to believe in yourself.
Say you can do anything you put your mind to,
Even if your mom has to remind you
When you ask for a job no one can decline you.

You overcome a lot of obstacles.
You wish you had done some things differently.
Like asking better questions than "Can I go pee?"
Hopefully you graduated and turned out successfully.

School is like a Prison

Jose Sandoval

School is like a prison.
We can't leave.

School is like an island.
We are all trapped.

School is like a pie.
It is good at first, until you reach the crust.

School is like a toilet.
It is full of germs.

School is like a salad.
You have to put something on it to make it better.

School is like a stupid cat.
It never dies.

School is like a garbage truck.
It smells, it's big, and you can hear it
From a mile away.

School is like a baby.
It always needs your attention.

School is like a shark.
It just keeps chasing.

School is like going to jail.
You never want to go back.

On The Dress Code

Zamani Lyde

Here come the teacher with the big fat...
Uh what's it stick or is she just a tick?
You're not allowed to wear that sweater, they say.
Only on a cold day, when they send us outside to play.

No one knows why I can't wear red nor gold.
Oh yeah, because it's not in dress code.
If they find my body on the dirt road,
Just tell them I died from the cold.

Another day another rule,
Another cruel...
Cruel what, oh yeah the rule is cruel.
Cruel to us, the ones who all drool.

School, school, school.
Lose the sweater, it's hot outside.
How about you enjoy the ride.
Cruel, cruel, cruel.

He Marches Into The Classroom

Alfredo Flores

He marches into the classroom.
Yelling and screaminmg, he.
His echoes come back.
Making my ears crack.

He.

He is the annoying fellow
Who screams his bellows.
He tries so hard to be me,
But he is not close to being me.

He calls me a hypocrite,
But knows I am innocent.
When he tries to find thesaurus,
Is like finding a tyrannosaurus.

He.

The Fellow Bellow.

Dress Code

Quinton Adams

There is no point in the dress code,
Especially if the kids who don't follow never get caught.
I try my best to follow dress code rules,
Otherwise teachers will give you detention, right on the spot.

Why is dress code so important?
Dress code in school it's just absolutely cray.
We have to follow it 95 percent of the time.
Can we have freedom, lean the scale our way?

Out of all colors, why the color white?
Or even the pants, which are about the color of crusty chains.
This was a horrible selection.
Really, who picked white? It is easily seen when it gets stained.

Do you get my point now?
The dress code shouldn't be.
Exactly what is the point of it?
Personally, I think the dress code
Should be banned for eternity.

Middle School

Julia Guo

Cars packed in front
Of my brand new school.
Old students, new students,
Friend students, and fiend students.

My old school was easier to get around,
Easier to relax in.

In the midst of my new classroom...
Lockers instead of cubbies.
New uniforms instead
Of new stylish outfits.
Gossiping about new girls
Instead of the excitement
Of seeing your elementary friends.

On my mind,
I think of the people in my class.
Four.
Literally only four of my elementary "friends"
Are in my class.

Another thought arises...
Was that girl just laughing at me?
Good, she's laughing at someone behind me...
Wait there's no one behind me!
Even though I'm getting annoyed
At her whispering and laughing at me...
I'll deal...

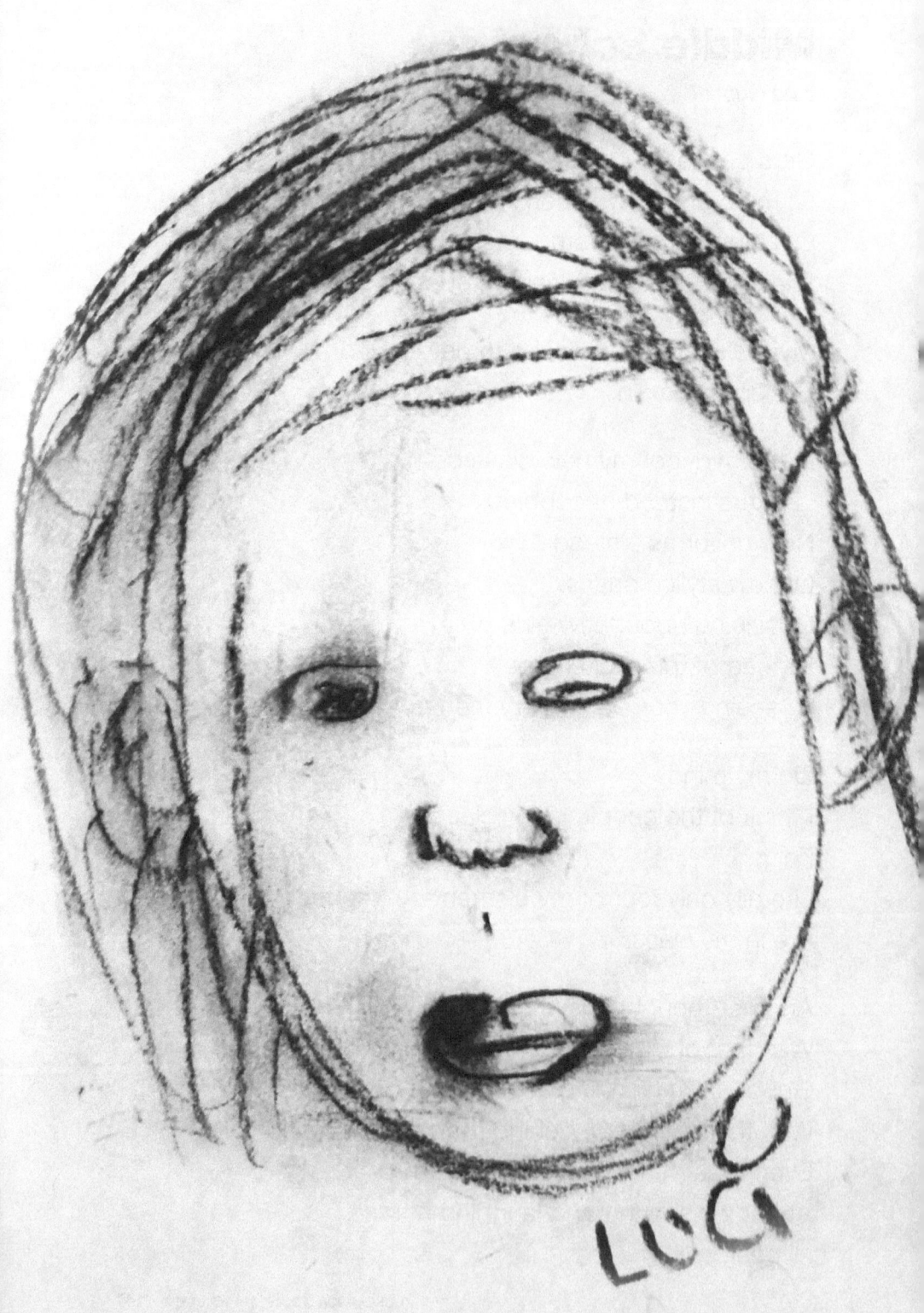

9 Holiday Musings

Iron Your Dress

Zamani Lyde

Iron your dress.
Curl your hair.
Don't have such a blank stare.
Truth is we're not all in despair.

Thanksgiving is here.
Why don't we all have one big cheer?
They sit, they eat, I sit and clear.
Clear my head of all the glare.

What shall I do?
Glue, clue, maybe a new shoe.
My mom makes pie, my dad make stew,
Cause it's just what they do.

Thanksgiving is here.
Why don't I care?
What shall I do? I have no clue.
But I do have a new shoe.

Thanksgiving, Creeping Up On me

Godwins Tuyishime

Thanksgiving, creeping up on me.
I have no intent.
A week of freedom and cheer,
Yet, excitement doesn't flood the mind.

Here it comes.
More killing for a simple holiday.
Turkeys run for their lives,
But not a chance of escaping.

More disconfort as well.
Excited to see your relatives, or are you?
"Oh, Great Aunt Annoying is coming again."
I'm pretty sure that's what's on our minds.

Thanksgiving, a day to give thanks.
Or is it another Halloween?
Another day of the dead,
And day of scares.

Christmas Is Coming

Devonte Alston

Christmas is coming.
In less than two months, it is.
The day of giving to others that are important.
Giving without expecting anything back.

At least
That's what is said.
What about that people who sacrificed?
Those people actually gave close to their lives.
In this day in time.

People end up dying on christmas.
Some of them gave their lives away.
All they got back were candles and flowers.
A beautiful scent that's not really there.

And a day, that celebrates a flying mammal.
When it comes to the giving,
The result will equal the taking as well.

Christmas

Ca'Shun Barr

Christmas.
It's the most wonderful time of the year.
Where Parents go broke,
For the price of their child's cheer.

But Santa is weird.
I'm talking deadly.
The guy stalks you 24/7.
Somehow, that's not an issue.
Honestly you should be afraid of this guy.

Shimmering down chimneys,
Eating all your cookies,
Drinking all your milk,
Somehow has the right to give you coal...

I think we should sign a petition.
Outlaw this creep.
Because, if this were your neighbor,
You
Wouldn't
Sleep.

Who Doesn't Like The Smell Of Cookies?

Trey Hensley

Who doesn't like smells of cookies?
Who doesn't like the presents?
Who doesn't like the frosty air of a Christmas morning?

Who doesn't like Christmas?
Waking up on a Christmas morning,
The time where if even you wake up at 5:00,
You'll wake your parents up and scream and yell.

Who doesn't enjoy the mornings?
The dinners,
Families come over,
Feasting on homemade traditional food that everyone enjoys.

Who doesn't enjoy the dinners?
The presents,
The best part of Christmas.
You've been waiting for 300 days to get
What you've wanted for ever.

They Say It's The Best Time Of Year

Samiyah Frasier

They said it's the best time of the year,
But if only they knew
What happens behind close doors.
Who will reveal the truth?

Hitting, kicking, screaming
Is what happens.
Would you stay to help me,
Or leave me all alone?

In the dark night,
When they abuse me,
When they start to torture me,
Will you?

Everything was perfect
I couldn't ask for anything more
But now, it's change...
Since its Christmas Day.

It's Coming

Godwins Tuyishime

It's coming.
The day of empty wallets and dying accounts.
The day for a baby wrapped in rag clothes,
Or a day to throw money away with no regret.

Children are ready for presents,
While parents, ready for the bankrupt letter.
"Papa's coming and I want lots of presents."
Well the mailman's coming, bringing lots of discontent.

"Well, I won't get anything, like usual"
And the next day, "check out my new stuff."
Disperse and disappointment.
Not uncommon for a day like this.

I still get a week off, and I get presents.
Well, check out the truth.
A day of fun.
More like a day of people that are done.

10 Heading West

Great-Grandpa Joe

Kayla Cannady

Growing up, Ma would always tell me tales of my great- grandfather Joe. I never knew him, but I felt from all I've heard about 'em, I knew him on a more personal level. One of my favorite tales was about his adventures during the westward expansion.

"Your great grandpa Joe was a pathfinder and a pioneer. He was known by the community to have great and strong nationalism and sectionalism no matter where he went." Ma explained.

I have always thought to myself on what great- grandpa was like. Was he all about the pioneer life? Did he ever go to those "old-timey" clubs called saloons or somethin'? I guess that will remain a mystery for now.

"He definitely loved his country and respected it very much. Grandpa Joe supported any annex since he loved the idea of being in new territory and land." Ma continued. "You know your great- grandpa Joe could be real confusin' sometimes. He didn't always want to be in those new areas, because everywhere he looked there was always a new doctrine that came about." She said.

"Oh wow, I see. Ma? Do you know what type of job great- grandpa had?" I asked.

"Well, when he wasn't too caught up in the concerns of new territory, he'd be at his job fixing locomotives. Dad told me that grandpa would converse with his workmates who disliked the thought of an annex. Boy, did their conversations heat up sometimes! But wise grandpa Joe would explain to them his thought of Manifest Destiny in hopes to secede them from their opinion. He was convincing alright." Ma continued with a little smirk plastered on her face.

"I wish I was as bold and courageous as him!" I said.

"Oh don't we all honey?" Ma replied.

I smiled back at her, and then asked her to proceed with the story.

"Grandpa was also an abolitionist. He believed that no matter what face or social status you were, you still should have suffrage. Not everyone felt the same way as him, and many even criticized him for it! Times were tough back them with all the injustice. Heck, it still is now!" Ma said with a little toughness in her voice.

She settled down some then started back where she left off. "Time had passed and eventually the new territory began to thrive. There were cowboys with their little colt revolvers and horses who started to come in the town. They'd go to a few popular saloons that they re-sorted at. When grandpa saw the saloons, he saw it as an opportunity for a higher paying job. You know, making a lot of money as a middle class man was scarce." She said with her head hanging low.

"So how did the saloon job work out?" I asked with curiosity.

"Well unfortunately Grandpa Joe didn't get hired. Turns out the manager had personal issues against him. He found out that Grandpa Joe supported equal rights for colored people, immigrants, and women. The manager highly disliked that, so Grandpa Joe never got the job. Turns out that was a good thing!" ma exclaimed.

"Why would that ever be a good thing Ma?" I won-dered.

"Around 6 months or so later, there was a gold rush out there west in California. Once he heard the news, sure enough he packed his things and headed out to Cali. His job there was a little risky depending on where they were searching for gold. He made some good money there, well at least better money compared to what he would make at the saloon." She said. "Your great grandpa Joe met your Great grandma Sally at a general store nearby his work. Your dad claims that he happened to get his charmer skills from Grandpa Joe. I highly doubted it, but if he got grandma Sally she must've saw something in him." Ma chuckled.

I chuckled along with her just thinking about G-grandpa's flirting skills.

"I wish he would be here to show me a few tricks here and there." I joked.

"Keep on wishin' Charles." she responded with a smile. "Well after he met Sally, they eventually got married and settled down. About three years later Grandma Sally had twin boys, Jim and my father Dan. Then a year later, she had my Aunt Deborah. Time went on from there and that is pretty much the story of how his adventures ended up with you and me." She concluded.

I sat for a while thinking on Grandpa Joe's adventures.

"Ma?" I asked.

"Yes sweetie?" she replied.

"Mind telling me some more adventures of Great-grandpa Joe?" I cheesed and asked all innocent like.

"Sure. You just love hearing about grandpa Joe, don't you?" she smiled.

"Sure do, Ma!" I smiled back.

The Day Aliens Attacked The West

Ayleen Galvan

"Sure is hot, ain't it?" Benny said lazily, while him and his friends rode their horses slowly through the desert.

"Yup." Said Tommy.

"Yup." Said Rosco.

"Yup." Said Jimmy.

"But it sure is nice, aint it?" Benny said.

"Yup" Said Tommy.

"Yup" Said Rosco.

"Sure would be nicer with a beer." Said Jimmy.

"Yup, I know a saloon down yonder, I could show you the way." Said Tommy.

"Alright then, lead the way, Tommy," Said Benny, backing up on his horse to let Tommy in front.

But as soon as Tommy got in the front of line. A mysterious blue beam shot from the sky, lifting Tommy higher and higher towards a gray disk amongst the clouds. Tommy's horse kicked and neighed but to no avail, Something was lifting Tommy and his horse!

"There's whisky in the sky?" Said Rosco.

"Rosco, ' ain't no time for jokes! Lasso him up like the cowboy you are!" Benny shouted. Benny, Jimmy and Rosco all took out their lasso ropes, and was able to catch him. But the blue grew wider and all four cowboys were being lifted up to their doom.

When they got to the top of the of beam, touching

the bottom of the flying disk, Jimmy knocked on the bottom and shouted, "Hey! You betta tell us what in tarnation is going on!" That bottom than opened up a hole for entrance, sucking the cowboys and their horses into the inside of the disk. When they got in, everything was stark white and had technology beyond their comprehension. Three equally white swivel chairs turned towards them. And the crew saw three small gray creatures with large heads and large almond black eyes. They wore sparkly orange suits, and stared back at the humans with a smile.

"Ayyyy " the creatures on the left said, "What is up, bruh?"

"Oh my goodness Kweku it's like 1851, they don't talk like that, idiot!" The creature in the middle said.

"But that's what my research said!" Kweku protested

"Well than you and your research are dumb!"

"Like your mum." Kweku mummbled, swiveling back around to press buttons on the machines...things.

Tommy brought up his colt revolver, and shot blindly at the monsters but they didn't flinch. Instead they laughed.

"We should probably introduce ourselves, I'm Xerox, this is Kweku and over here is Xxyyzz_138_XD, but you can call him XD for short."

"Our species, the Wubberoos, cannot be harmed by simple bullets, in fact, it is required to wear a pain proof suit when visiting Earth, as humans tend to mindlessly hurt things they don't understand." Explained XD.

The cowboys trembled in fear. They could hardly understand what the creatures were saying, much less their situation. When Rosco turned around to where his horses were, he found them gone.

"Hey! Where are our horses?" Rosco said to the creatures, and the other guys turned around and saw that their horses are gone, too. They all started shouting. Xerox brought out his high tech laser gun and shot in the air. Bleep Bloop!

The men shut up. And listened to what Xerox had to say.

"I was just getting to that part, as you can see, our race, the Wubberoos do not come in peace, we plan to annex the south to be our new habitat. But first we have to make sure humans are not smart enough to see through our technology. From what I've seen so far, the Wubberoos have nothing to worry about."

"W-what does that means, Benny?" Whispered Tommy

"I think it means we're in a whole lotta trouble if we don't pass this test of theirs." Benny whispered.

The Wubberoos explained their plan for a loooong, time. Something about a doctrine, but the men only half listened. When they were done, the men were zapped into a new environment.

"Where are we?" Rosco asked, confused by everything around him. Their was black gravel where the dirt used to be, and colorful locomotives zooming at paces much faster than their horses combined. The sidewalk was made with gray rock, and not wood. And the air smelled oily and rancid.

"We're in the future dumbos, we're cha listenin'?" Jimmy responded.

"How was I supposed to listen with all those... those... critters and space stuff!" Jimmy argued.

"Well, we're supposed to find our horses, reckon theys somewhere 'round here." He continued.

"Maybe, their in that shoppe over there!" Said Benny, pointing to a gas station across the street.

"Well how we there? There's a big ole road in front of us!" Said Rosco.

"We cross, stupid!" Yelled Benny.

The aliens watched over the cowboys with great interest.

"Kweku, where did you put the horses? You scattered them out right?" Asked Xerox.

"No. They're all in the convenience store like you told me to put them."

"You what! You were supposed to spread them out, you stupid glipglop!"

"Well you thought all my other ideas were stupid. And no need to call me the g word, I'm not that gray."

"Well you're ideas were stupid, Gold Rush and Manifest Destiny? That's like, already happening!"

"Do not make me bust off at you."

The cowboys below crossed the road, but with difficulty. When they got to the gas station, the talked to a man with a car that said, 'pathfinder'.

"Howdy, pathfinder! We got a bit of trouble and we need some help." Benny greeted the man.

The man looked up from putting gas in his car.

"What in the world..." He mumbled.

"Have ya seen any horses around here? Me and my friends need to get back home."

"Ummm... Actually yeah, there was horses in the store, for some reason." he said.

The cowboys ran towards the store, almost shattered the glass doors coming in, and found their horses. The men whooped and hollered and hugged their horses. As soon as they touched their horses, they were lifted into the air and found themselves back in the flying disk. Xerox did not look happy.

This time no-one really listened, but they laughed when Kweku got smacked and called a glipglop again. They were transported back to their time, much to the Wubberoos disapproval. And the cowboys lived happily ever after.

"We're still going to inhabit Earth right?" Asked XD after they dropped of the humans.

"Yeah, but let's go to Florida, the people there are waaay too dumb to notice us." Said Kweku.

"Florida it is than, let's go." Commanded Xerox. And their spaceship zoomed off to Florida.

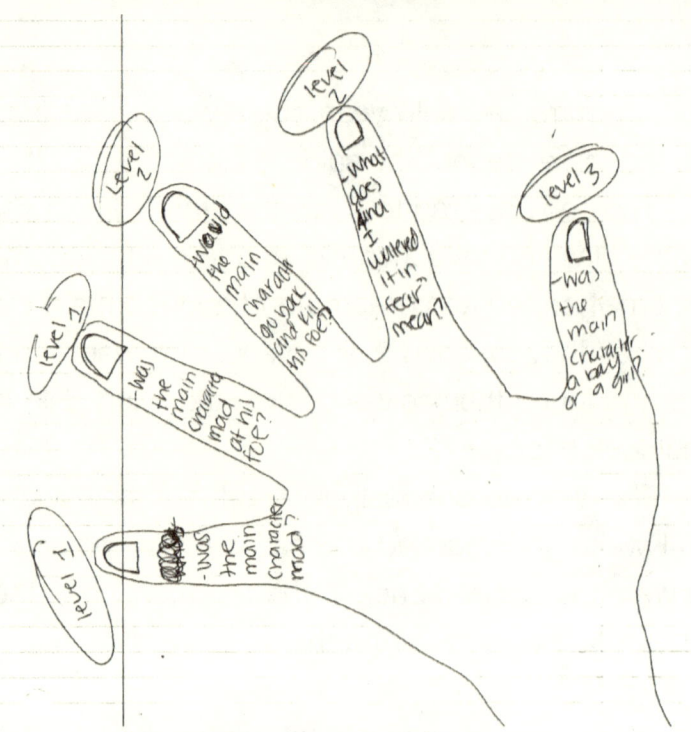

Sunny West Treasure

Matthew K. Greene

In the world of coal, there was never gold or diamonds. To the people, it was only in dreams. Some people thought gold and diamonds were found in sunny, hot paradises. Some people still believe the legend.

Scotch lived in Ireland. He lived in a dirty redhead Irish village. He was a poor man. Food was so scarce to find. Not a person wanted to help him, only because he was a peasant. However that did not stop him from living day by day on the little food he had. He had no one to even love or depend on.

Futt was a man who roamed his country. He did not love his home because there was not enough opportunities. He depended on his mind and the chances he had.

One day when Futt walked home, he saw Scotch dying slowly. He gave Scotch the opportunity to secede from his poverty life. Later, they took a ride on top of the locomotive to get to the stronger man, the leader.

The Pathfinder was a proud man who was into nationalism. He was a man with pride for his country that he wanted to spread the Irish love and culture. Futt asked if they could be an annex. They wanted to be a part of the list to the new land.

The pathfinder declined their suggestion/begging because he was in a doctrine group. The group would not allow them to be a passenger because of their low rank status in society. Everyone was allowed to go to the new land because they were in the lower class. Scotch was determined to adapt to sectionalism they reached to the supposed land.

Days later, they snuck onto the Irish ship. They traveled with some of the Pioneers who lead them to California.The crew finally reached their Manifest Destiny. All were fortunate to getting fifty acres of soil per person. Most people lived in the deep sunny west because of the legend. But for years there was no gold or treasure.

For five years Scotch and Futt's lives changed. They had become beloved cowboys. They were also safe by carrying colt revolvers with them. They were happy less poor living people.

As often or most of the time they visited the Vex Saloon to relax. They became in great debt for their order. And if they did not say it of in less than twenty four hours they would be killed shot down by Vex himself. For now, they were banned from the saloon until they died.

They went to their separated home. Futt got so mad he ended up shooting towards the sun. Yellowish metal fell from the sun's side. Gold! Futt and Scotch retrieved the gold and went to pay their debt to Vex.

Vex yelled out on the scene of payment that their part of land had the legendary yellow metal. Scotch and Futt became abolitionist to that idea. Suffrage, they all voted to invade their home and land.

The townspeople finally decided to go collect some gold from their land. It was a gold rush invasion. All people from the world came. None found nothing until a child noticed the crack on the sun's skin. The gold was on the sun.

Most townspeople used ladders to get to the sun for they did not know one could shoot at the sun. When they finally reached the sky it became night time. The moon was so close you could notice that it had the legendary diamonds.

Men used their utensils to remove the diamonds. Most diamonds that were removed would float into the night sky and the rest would fell deep into the ground.

They would dig and climb for years. The climbers would usually fall to their deaths. And the diamonds diggers would usually dig to their own grave.

Meanwhile Scotch and Futt had had gotten enough gold for the rest of their life. Their hard work and determination was rewarded. They bought two horses, one brown and the other black. They rode off to a better life and a new home or paradise with their sunny west treasure.

Gray

11 They Say, I Say

They Say, I Say

Jonathan V. Chavez

They say I'm a wetback.
I say
I'm better than you.

They say I steal your jobs.
I say
I know how to do what you lazy wejos can't do,
So
Don't judge me by how much better I am than you.

They say I'm not worth being in America.
I say
Stop trying to be jealous.
Instead,
I'm going to prove you wrong,
To make you look way dumber than you already are.

They Say, I Say

Anthony Velasquez

They say we're aliens.
I say
I am human.

They say we're lazy.
I say
I know how to work,
So
Don't judge me by my color.

They say we're a disgrace to this nation.
I say
I am helpful to this nation.

They say I'm not part of this society.
I say
Stop discrimination.
Instead,
I'm gonna get an education
To help my people.

They Say, I Say

A'munique Syas

They say I'm not going anywhere.
I say
I am going to get there.

They say I will never prosper.
I say
I am going to be a doctor,
So
Don't judge
My future by my past.

They say I'm dumb.
I say
I'm smart.

They say I'm not going to make it.
I say
Stop with all the hatred.
Instead
I'm gonna get the knowledge
To get to college.

They Say, I Say

Leroy Brown

They say I am dumb.
I say
I am smart.

They say I can't do stuff.
I say
I know how to handle situations better,
So
Don't judge me by
The way I think.

They say I'm not
Going to do nothing in the world.
I say
Stop saying I can't make it.

Instead
I'm gonna get my degree
To help build my future.

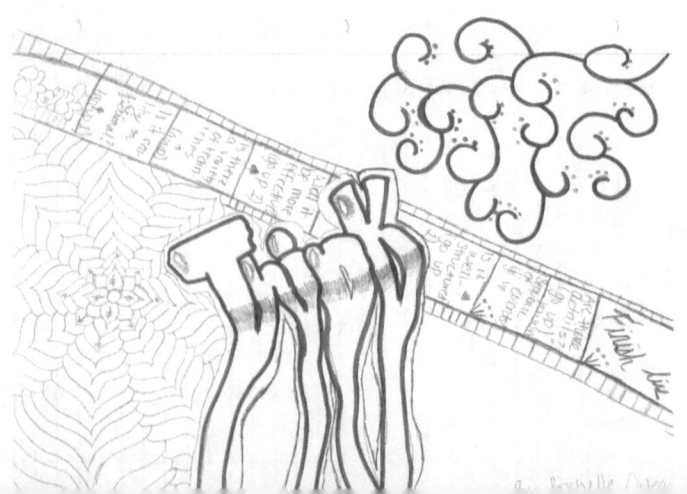

They Say, I Say

William Brown

They say I'm not the best.
I say
I am great.

They say I can't achieve.
I say
I know how to believe,
So
Don't judge me by what you see.

They say I'm not cool.
I say
Stop judging me you fool.

Instead,
I'm gonna ignore you and keep on going
To keep growing.

They Say, I Say

Qui-yon Richards

They say I am black.
I say
I am smart.

They say I don't know how to work.
I say, I know how to go to church.

So,
Don't judge me
By the cover of my book.

They say I'm not good enough,
Because of the color of my face.
I say, stop being jealous,
Because you want my place.

Instead I'm gonna
Take the education that I learn today
To help make the world a better place.

They Say, I Say

Kyah Halston

They say I am ugly and fat.
I say I am flawless.

They say I am stupid.
I say I know how to READ.
So don't judge me by what you hear or
See.

They say I am talkative.
I say you don't speak much at all.

They say I'm not going to be anything in
Life.
I say STOP hating on the best.

Instead, I'm going to be a
Pediatrician to help save
Your children.

They Say I Say

Quinton Adams

They say it will end like many others.
I say
I am a book so I don't judge me by my
cover.

They say I am afraid of fear.
I say
I know how to work diligently
So
Don't judge me by the way I appear.

They say upon myself I will only bring stress.
I say
I am the very thing that will bring me
success.

They say I'm not gonna make it out
And have complete strife.
I say
Stop with the insults because I know in this life
I will succeed.

Instead,
I'm gonna tell myself I will never quit.
To know in my mind that I will always make it.

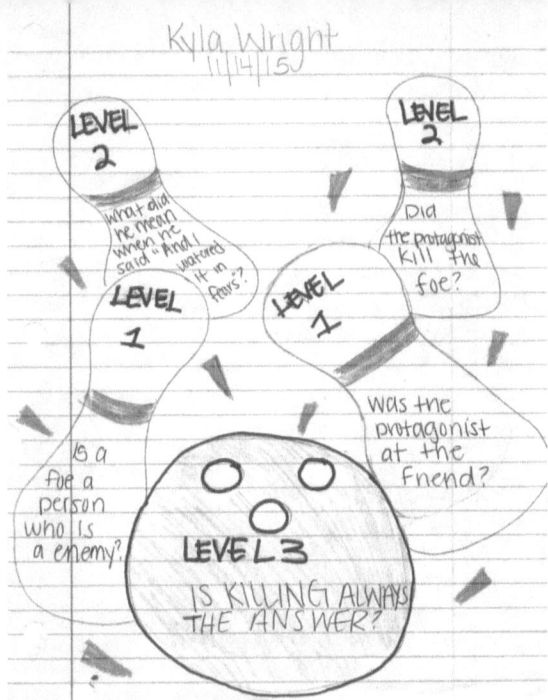

They Say, I Say

Nathaniel Skinner

They say I am too tall
I say my height matches my dreams.

They say I am too young,
I say I am wise beyond my years.
So don't judge me by the way I look
Or how old I am.

They say great minds think alike,
I say great minds think by themselves.

They say
Reach for the stars.
I say
Go beyond the galaxy.

They Say, I Say

Syemone Horlbeck

They say I am ugly.
I say
I am pretty.

The say I'm a follower.
I say
I know how to be a leader,
So don't judge me by looking at me.

They say I am ugly.
I say I am beautiful.

They say I'm not going to be anybody in this world.
I say
Stop looking at me
And judging me
Just by looking at me.

Instead,
I'm going to succeed in the world,
To be an inspiration to my sisters.

Full of drama

Natavia Goodwin

They say I'm full of drama.
I say
I'm like my mama.

They say I'm easy going.
I say
I know how to keep it flowing.
So
Don't judge me by
What you've heard.

They say I like to eat.
I say
I'm pretty neat.

They say I'm not going to make a difference
I say
Stop guessing.

Instead,
I'm gonna make a difference
To change my world.

12 Journeys

I am

Darren Montgomery

I am from a potato, from a hot box and McCallisters.

I am from the cold, hard, and smelly.

I am from the root of the ground, flat fields,
and freshly cut grass.

I am from praying at dinner, and dancing from
uncle bug and trell and Angelique.

I am from a loving and caring family -
from don't do drugs and be respectful.

I am from a baptist church and Christians.

I am from Charleston - seafood - from the shoes
in my grandmother's closet the clothes and jewelry
on my aunt's dresser.

I am from the family room, wall of fame
including honor roll and outstanding achievements.

It's Almost Over

Godwins Tuyishime

It's almost over.
The cold year of pain,
The hell in the icy room of that man.
Not only that, we burn at home, like acid rain.

One down, three to go.
May seem like a lot more,
But I aint done, no.
I got a long way to go, but
I'll breeze my way through.

I'm tired of the cold winter.
Can't wait for me to me a winner,
To graduate from that stage
And join my beautiful age.

One down, three to go.
I'll keep counting till the end.
Next time, it will be done.
Four down now it's done.

Failure

Samiyah Frasier

They said I couldn't make it.
They said I wouldn't make it.
And they were right.
I couldn't.

I don't have accomplishments.
I don't have goals.
I don't have pride.
I don't have dignity.
I don't have anything.

Where did everything go?
There's nothing there.
I can't find it.
I am just pathetic.

I am just worthless.
Why do people acknowledge me?
I am not a survivor.
I am a failure.

I Am Not Perfect

Rochelle Ortega

I am not perfect.
I have yet to fall.
I will pick myself up with my feet,
And not let anyone top me.

I am me, so I do not care.
If you think I am nonperfect,
I am me,
And that will not flee.

I am not perfect,
And so aren't you.
But I know what I am not.
And you have yet to know.

I will grow to be an amazing person.
But you,
You will be acting like you're perfect.
I can see the ways I am not perfect,
But they make me
Me.

We Are All The Same

Rochelle Ortega

We are all the same.
No matter what the race,
You can be black, white, yellow, or red.
On the inside we are all the same.

People say one race is inferior,
But I think otherwise.
I think one race is just as inferior as the other.
We are all the same on the inside.

We are just as great as the other.
No one is better than another.
I am not inferior & neither is the other.
I am just as good as a white, black, tan,
Or dark skinned person.

A white man is no better than a black man.
A rich white women might be richer in economy.
But what matters is the heart.
With no heart you have nothing.

The Dark Sins Of Me

Kyeara Grate

Anger - Oh, How compromising you are!
Jealousy - Busted the windows out his car.
Lust - Leads to my past of untrust.
Depression - Always teaches me a lesson.
Greed - Gets my wants mixed up with needs.

Don't need any apologies.
Don't need you to demolish me.
Don't need nobody to sit and stare.
Don't need anybody who wasn't there.

Just remember me,
Like you always do.
While you feeling the fire,
I am keeping cool.

Funny, I remembered how you looked, too.
Almost like a million bucks.
Wait, Scratch that- Not a million bucks.

You just looked
Like a piece of dust
With a hint
Of bad luck.

He's My Best Friend

Rochelle Ortega

He's my best friend.
He knows me better
Than I know myself.
I love him.

I love him for who he is,
No matter what others say.
He's part of my family.
He's part of me.

Without him I cannot live.
He knows everything there is to know,
And even more.
He simply completes my life.

He's like a brother in a way,
But not completely.
He might be male,
But he knows what I feel.

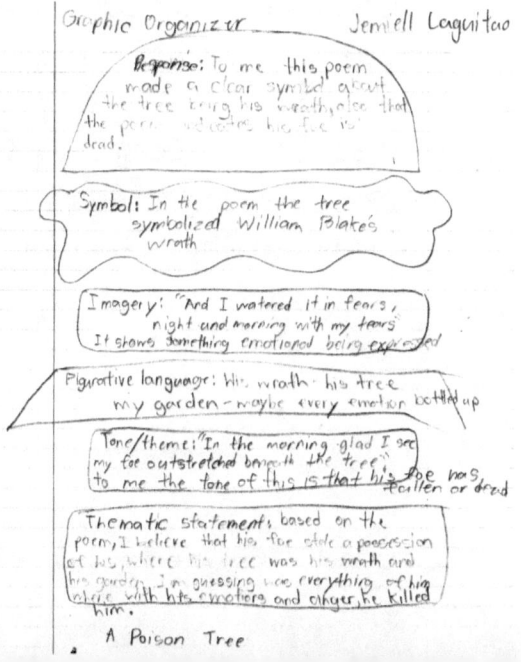

Graphic Organizer   Jenniell Laguitao

Response: To me this poem
made a clear symbol about
the tree being his wrath, also that
the poem indicates his foe is
dead.

Symbol: In the poem the tree
symbolized William Blake's
wrath

Imagery: "And I watered it in fears,
night and morning with my tears"
It shows something emotional being expressed

Figurative language: His wrath, his tree,
my garden - maybe every emotion bottled up

Tone/theme: "In the morning glad I see
my foe outstretched beneath the tree"
to me the tone of this is that his foe has
fallen or dead

Thematic statements: based on the
poem, I believe that his foe stole a possession
of his, where his tree was his wrath and
his garden - im guessing was everything of his
also with his emotions and anger, he killed
him.

A Poison Tree

Mother

Kory Singleton

When he was a boy,
He was robbed of his joy.
So he went away and he dreamed all night.
He dreamed of sun, sun, sunlight.

The person to brighten up his life.
He wanted to feel really light.
Not carry the planet, relieve that strife.
It was him, his father, and the frozen sea.

He wonders "Why does the sun mean so much to me?"
He needed something to brighten up his world.
He needed that warmth and feeling of protection.
He knew who he was.
But didn't know who could be his sun in the sky.

Years passed and moved away.
A way... A way towards peace and happiness.
He found the literal heat.
But couldn't overcome the grief.
When the sight of a certain tombstone struck his heart,
And realized why he kept it in the dark.

Light and Darkness

Brennen Kieffer

The darkness is the enemy of the world.
It will break your spirit.
It will torture your soul.
This is your worst fear.

The light is everyone's hope.
It shall guard and protect you.
It will not leave your side.
It is the guardian of the world.

The world is full of
 light and darkness.

They are but two forces.
Each balances out the other.
There must not be just light,
And there must not be just darkness.

Only one is superior.
Darkness or light .
Who will it be?
No one knows...

Before You Start To Stare

Kyeara Grate

I see you staring at me,
Thinking "Ooh there she go,"
I got the whole crowd staring.
Just call me a pro.

Rounds of applause
Is all I hear.
Got everybody in my face,
From ear to ear.

Trying to stop.
Honey, I can't be beat.
Whenever I get around you,
Your boyfriend feels the heat.

Flipping and Whipping my hair,
Without a single care.
Just remember to look beside you,
Before you start to stare.

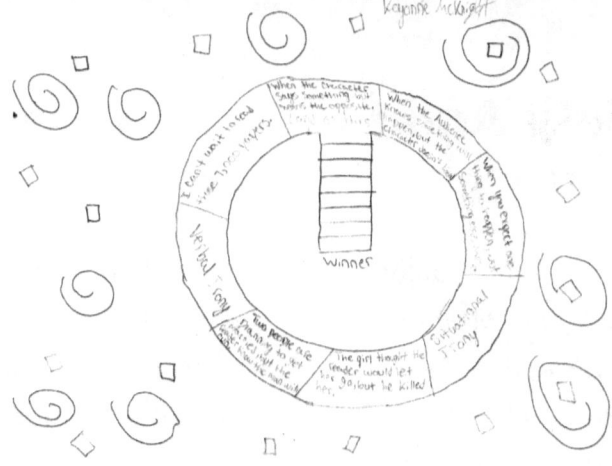

Home

Belen Martinez

I stepped in the building.
I was scared, I was nervous.
I remember a teacher walking me to class.
There I was, entering Ms. Macomber's room.

She made me feel so welcomed,
With a big cheesy smile,
And her beautiful red hair.
I felt like if I was home.

Now I'm in 8th grade, I feel the same way
That I've felt since 6th grade,
Which is good.

I feel safe.
I feel warm.
I feel cozy in my school,
Which is home.

Society And I

Jalynn Henryhand

I look in the mirror lately,
Trying to figure what does
Society want from me.
What can I be?

Too far from the truth
I am.
For I'm not perfect
Nore can I pretend.

Though I shed tear
I can't…
I don't won't to fix it.
I can't fix the lie.

Society is a lie.
I'm a bigger one.
Lies keep me safe,
Keep me careful.

Careful of those who hurt.
Pretend to be the best,
For I'm not
Nor will I pretend to be.

Society moves on,
I don't.
Strong emotions I carry.
Weak thoughts are society.

Only to crush.
Crush what they can't have.
Reality.
I'm a fairy tale.

Waiting to be shared,
Recognized,
Brought to life.
Society is a nightmare.

No one wakes up,
No one leaves…
No one leaves…
We can't leave.

I can't leave my lies.
My pain.
My reality.
I only wait. It will happen.

Society and I will happen

Broken

Tristan Fryer

Broken, stone at your feet,
Bat, blood, around his head,
Cold nights, gangs, drugs, alcohol,
All you could want, right?

Home

Daniel Hernandez

Many people say I am not from LA.
They say I am from Charleston.
Well if you really know me,
You know I'm from Compton.

I'm from the inner city.
The Hub city.
I'm part of NWA.
I'm friends with K.Dot, Dre and the Game.

The place where gangs and drugs rule the world.
The place where you see hookers and girls.
The crack separated the families.
Back in the 1990's.

People consider this place hell.
I consider it home.
Because at the end of the day,
This is Compton.

Back to Society

Kenny Coronel

All of her walls are broken
From reality that she has awoken.
She was building a wall
To protect her from all.

Isolation, as you could say,
So that she could stay
In her own world,
Where she twirled.

Under her own spotlight,
Until twilight,
Where she wasn't bothered.
The only place that she felt honored.

Truth is, that wasn't reality.
It just wasn't the normality.
For her, it was home,
Where she spent her days alone.

She finally went back to society.
All she could feel was anxiety,
Where she could be discriminated.
Or worse— she could be eliminated.

A Hero

Jessica Bevins

A hero is someone who protects,
Not just someone in tight leather pants.
They don't shoot lasers and fly.
It's someone who you can call on
In a hopeless and stressful time.

They don't have super speed or indescribable strength.
They use their bare hands even if it's a big risk.
They care about others that person could be you.
You could even be a hero the choice is up to you.

A hero can be an inspiration to you.
They could inspire you to help someone in need.
Don't be afraid to be a hero.
There could be a blessing you could receive.
You could be an inspiration to someone.
That's all they could need.

How do you become a hero? It's easy if you believe.
Help someone who is homeless.
You could be the blessing they need.
Give them money or buy something they need.
You'll never know how much joy they will receive.

You could also be a hero by volunteering somewhere.
Try a nursing home and help the elderly.
You could make them feel special

When some families didn't care.
Be the family member that didn't care show them.
The compassion love and care that was never there.

By fundraising, you could be an awsome hero.
Raise money for cancer or diabetes.
You could save someone's life by the money you give.
So be a hero today and don't let trials come your way.
By being the hero you are you could be
The best person of them all.

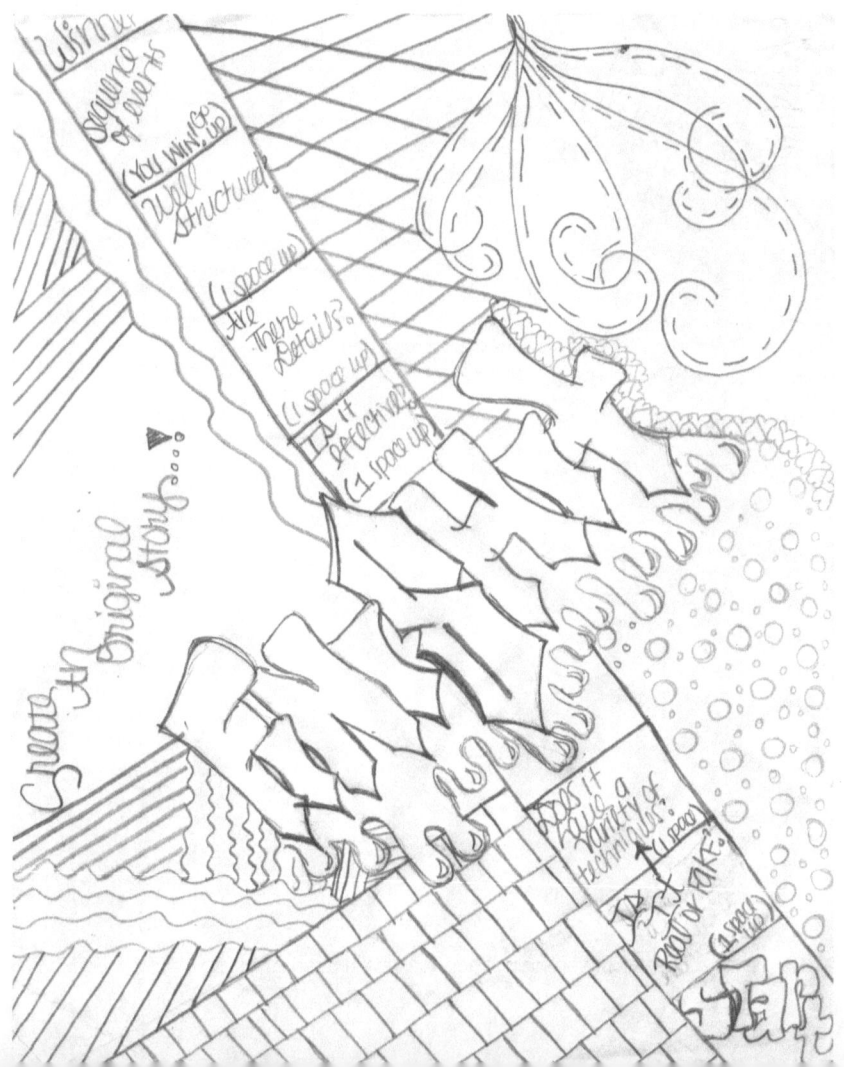

Epilogue

Someone far more interesting that I once said that the only thing that can stop an unstoppable force is an inmovable object. And I suppose that might be true, though in my experience I have not personally encountered either. I can say that I have seen some of these qualities in this latest issue of Zuckerbook – Open It And Read, and this makes me terribly proud.

Last year, when the second volume of Zuckerbook was produced by a ragtag group of ingenius students who worked together under duress, with various degrees of involvement and interest, I have to say that I had my doubts about producing a new issue. How could another group of students be assembled that could snap together another issue, loaded with new material, new artwork, new inspiration, and new stories, possibly form from the ether that is the upcoming year? I had no idea. I still don't. We were all flying by the seats of our pants, a crew of newbies (myself included), lighting out for unexplored territory, learning about publishing and business and fundraising and sales and anything else you could pile on, none of us really having any idea how to do what we were doing but determined as all get out to get it done and produce something that had never been done before in a middle school in our area... as far as we knew. Big plans were thrown together about publishing twice over the oncoming school year, more involvement from faculty, more involvement from a more diverse collection of students, some sort of distribution that went beyond a weekly run to the post office and frantically stuffed envelopes, and a largely ignored GoFundMe page (that URL remains on the back cover of this book, just in case you are feeling altruistic). We had to get into the game, somehow, but how would we do it?

I had no real ideas on that one, having tried sales before and failed miserably, but I knew some people who knew some people who had had a measure of success, and that was better than nothing. There were meetings with folks that make money for other folks, accountant people who knew numbers better than I (easy, really, part of why I teach English), people who specialized in brand identity, and the like. All of it was terribly informative, and all of it pointed to the need for a far leaner and more specialized staff of students who were precocious, a little cheeky, very intelligent, and driven to take Zuckerbook and The Zuckerbook Project to the next level.

We had a lot of people on staff last year, and there were a lot of times when several of them had nothing to do, having already completed their jobs. They tried, of course, to find something more to do…most of them, anyway…but still, the class was too big and unspecialized. We needed to be lean. Mean. A literary fighting machine. So, after a few nonchalant discussions with last year's staff, I whittled eighteen students down to eleven, gave them very specific jobs and duties, and hoped for the best.

We organized into three teams: Marketing, in charge of developing and maintaining our brand identity, developing advertising, and developing graphics for our various advertising outlets; Internal Production, in charge of editing submitted material, organizing submissions into categories, and selecting artwork; and Public Relations, who were now in charge not only of press releases, but also social media: Facebook, Pinterest, Instagram, Twitter, Snapchat, and our own website, which includes information on where our profits go (we donate to DonorsChoose.org grants for our faculty and sports programs), a blog on our daily happenings, and information on ways to buy our work. We also took on a Chief Financial Officer, who kept track of sales, the various challens we have for donations, income, expenses, and accounting. She also kept track of the other team leaders, grading them each week on their performance, and they, in turn, graded their team members based on productivity. I, as you do, when you have the chance, hung out, wrote lesson plans, gave instructions, guided, and hoped for the best.

I am not disappointed. Not in the least. By and large, these kids jumped right in, demonstrated the sort of enthusiasm it takes to succeed, and really went for it. I am a darned proud teacher, and excited for our future.

Speaking of the future, it looks pretty bright for us. We have managed to get a few book distributors interested in helping us market Zuckerbook, and (ideally) our future publications. Barnes and Noble have ordered twenty-five copies of our last edition, and (ideally) will order more of our work. We are looking at publishing at least twice this year, starting with this volume, and may also publish an annual anthology of student short stories, expanding our author base to include former students of Zucker Middle School. We also have a few former students who have decided to write novels approach us for assistance in getting their work into print and into stores, and we could not be more happy to assist them. A remark-able amount of talent wanders through the halls of that school, and it is about time that the world had an opportunity to see what they bring to the table.

It is a very well laid spread, a veritable feast. I hope you all enjoy it as much as we have. If you are ever in North Charleston, drop us a line, or stop on by. We would love to visit.

With grattitude, a tip of the hat, and a big ol' smile,

Erik J. Hilden
November 26th, 2015

www.ingramcontent.com/pod-product-compliance
Lightning Source LLC
Chambersburg PA
CBHW031415250626
47155CB00004B/1503